WORLD AIRLINE COLOURS

By Nigel M. Tomkins

London • England

Published by
Aviation Data Centre Ltd,
Browcom House,
Browells Lane,
Feltham, Middlesex,
TW13 7EQ, England.

ISBN: 0 946141 16 9

Printed in Great Britain by:

Intergraphic Print (UK) Ltd,
Browcom House, Browells Lane, Feltham, Middlesex, TW13 7EQ, England.

INTRODUCTION

Welcome to the first edition of World Airline Colours, an exciting new publication which provides a unique reference to the liveries of some 148 of the world top airlines. Ultimately we intend to produce a total of four volumes of this work which will comprehensively detail the 600 world airlines that display a recognised colourscheme, but within this edition we have chosen to include primarily airlines based in or visiting Europe ranging from international flag carriers to domestic charter operators and including aircraft types from the mighty Boeing 747-300 to the tiny Bandeirante and Twin Otter. Each airline's entry includes a brief write-up covering history, type of operations, aircraft types operated and colourscheme background, as well as a colour illustration of a typical fleet member wearing the company's current livery. The illustrations have been supplied as colour transparencies by many of the world's top aviation photographers and are all original, never having appeared in any other publications in a similar form. A comprehensive cross-reference index is incorporated at the back of the book to assist the reader in locating airlines included. The airline colourscheme world, the subject of this book, is indeed rapidly changing and even as we go to press we learn of three proposed new liveries that will be adopted by airlines covered in this issue in the near future, British Midland, Balkan and Transavia but these will appear in subsequent issues as they are applied to aircraft. We hope that you will enjoy reading and referring to this edition as much as we have enjoyed compiling it, and will stay with us through the next three volumes and subsequent update issues.

ACKNOWLEDGEMENTS

We would like to express our sincere thanks to all the top aviation photographers who supplied examples of their work for inclusion in this first edition, particularly the following:

Christian Volpati, Christian Laugier, Dario Cocco, Marcel Walther, Philippe Petit, George Ditchfield, Richard Vandervord, Gerald McLaughlin, Stephane Salandre, Martin Hornliman, Henk Boele, Charles Bargibant, Mikkel Morbech, Jean-Luc Altherr, Maurice Bertrand, Michael Steinlein, Conti Eugenio, Damiano Gualdoni, Michele Vandaele, Malcolm Nason, A. J. M. Hofstra, Philippe Collet, Chris Green, Keith Gaskell, Antonio Branca, Norbert Heck, Jerry Stanick, Chris Mak, Ron Mak, A. Senziani, Udo Weisse, Scott Meredith, Kazuhiro Murai, Wolfgang Hut, Simon Wills, Flemming Lovenvig, Denis Fleury, Christian Sparr, Adolfo Tagliabue, Frank De Koster, Svante Nyholm, Luc Bereni, Ron Kluk, Mickey Bednar, Glen Auld, John Blatherwick, J. V. D. Heijden.

The above list reads like a who's who of the aviation photography world and we very much hope that they and other quality slide photographers will contribute examples of their work for the second volume in the series.

AER LINGUS

The national airline of the Republic of Ireland was originally formed on May 22nd 1936 by the Irish Government, with the technical assistance of Blackpool and West Coast Air Services, to operate a single de Havilland Dragon to Bristol, eventually merging with the international Aerlinte Eireann which was itself formed in 1947. The two companies were fully integrated and the resulting Aer Lingus now maintains an impressive scheduled passenger and freight route network linking the Republic with cities in the United Kingdom, Europe and the United States.

Aer Lingus has been well served by its fleet of Boeing 737s and plans to use them for the forseeable future, possibly enhanced by some of the new -300 series. A few British Aerospace One-Elevens and Shorts 360s are used on the secondary routes with wide-bodied Boeing 747s on the long haul and high density services.

The company livery, designed by King and Wetherell, reflects a bold national identity through the use of predominantly green colouring and Irish Shamrock logos. The fuselage displays a distinctive bright green roof and dark green windowline, separated by a band of bright blue, with the lower section in white and the belly in grey. A simple Shamrock is worn on the fin in white, and repeated alongside the 'Aer Lingus' fuselage lettering in bright green.

Boeing 737-248 EI-ASA.

AEROFLOT

Numerically the largest airline in the world, Aeroflot is the state-owned national carrier of the Soviet Union. The company is charged with operating not only an extensive scheduled domestic and international network, but also operations such as firefighting, crop spraying, air ambulance, in fact all civilian aircraft in Russia fly under the Aeroflot banner.

Naturally a vast fleet is needed and this consists of examples of every Soviet built transport aircraft ranging from the massive new Antonov An-124 to smaller types such as the Antonov An-2, including Antonov An-12s, An-22s, An-24s, An-26s, An-30s, An-72s, Ilyushin Il-14s, Il-18s, Il-62s, Il-76s, Il-86s, LET Turbolets, Tupolev Tu-134s, 154s, Yakolev YAK-40s and 42s, plus considerable numbers of various helicopters.

The standard livery used includes a dark blue windowline, trimmed below by a dark blue pinstripe, leading from front to rear, with a plain Soviet flag dominating the white tail. The airline is identified by 'Aeroflot' titling in dark blue cyrillic script only, making it one of the few carriers not to include English titles. The most notable variation to the livery is worn by domestic aircraft which tend to have a much smaller tail flag.

Ilyushin IL-76M CCCP-86826 at Paris. (Christian Volpati)

AEROLINEAS ARGENTINAS

The flag-carrier of the South American republic of Argentina was formed in 1949 and has expanded to the point where it now flies to Europe, Africa, North America and South America, as well as providing numerous domestic flights to destinations within Argentina.

The large fleet comprises mostly Boeing jets, 727-200s and 737-200s with 747s used on long-haul services and a few Dutch-built Fokker Fellowships on the shorter routes.

All fleet members wear an identical livery which features twin cheatlines in medium and dark blue, extending from the nose, widening along the fuselage, and terminating on the fin, where each is topped by a similarly coloured 'A' initial. Dark blue 'Aerolineas Argentinas' titles are carried on the forward fuselage, as is the traditional bird logo, now a secondary feature of the scheme.

Boeing 747-287B LV-OPA at Paris-Orly. (Christian Laugier)

AERO TRANSPORTI ITALIANI - ATI

An associate company of Alitalia, ATI was formed in December 1963 as the Italian domestic passenger airline to take over the services of Societa Aerea Mediterranea -SAM. The company's scheduled passenger route network now includes over twenty cities on the Italian mainland as well as the islands of Pantelleria and Lampedusa. ATI also offers passenger charters, since 1974, mainly bringing holidaymakers to Italy from other parts of Europe, and is expected to be merged with sister company Aermediterranea in the near future.

The present fleet is based on twenty-one McDonnell Douglas DC-9-32s with delivery of twelve McDonnell Douglas MD-82s well advanced. Shorter sectors are served by Fokker Friendships, due to be replaced by new Aeritalia/Aerospatiale ATR-42s.

ATI's livery is largely based on that of Alitalia, underlining the companies' close ties, with the windowline forming a large stylised 'A' initial on the tail but in dark blue and light blue instead of Alitalia's green and red. If anything, the ATI scheme is even more attractive than that of Alitalia, with its foreshortened cheatline allowing for a more dynamic logo which takes up most of the forward fuselage. Note the black nose-tip, a feature common to all aircraft in the ATI and Alitalia fleets.

McDonnell Douglas DC-9-32 I-DIZO at Linate. (Dario Cocco)

AIR AFRIQUE

AIR AFRIQUE was formed in March 1961 as a multi-national venture with the involvement of Cameroon, Central African Republic, Chad, Congo-Brazzaville, Dahomey, Gabon, Ivory Coast, Mauritania, Niger, Senegal and Upper Volta, to pool the resources of each nation for the funding of an international airline. The organisation has been changed in subsequent years with Togo and Sierra Leone joining and Gabon and Cameroon leaving, but has worked remarkably well and now provides regional scheduled passenger and freight services throughout Central and West Africa, and northerly to Europe and North Africa, as well as flying to New York.

Four Douglas DC-8s, two Aerospatiale Caravelles and two leased Boeing 727-200s are used on regional routes augmented by wide-bodied Airbus Industrie A300s, with a Boeing 747 and three McDonnell Douglas DC-10s flying further afield.

With so many nationalities involved, it was logical that the livery of Air Afrique should make use of neutral colours, so bright shades of lime and emerald green were chosen to colour the broad cheatlines. Simple 'Air Afrique' titles are displayed on the white roof in black upper case lettering, but the livery's centrepiece is the ethnic tail logo which symbolises far reaching services by the use of a Gazelle's head spanning a stylised globe, in a matching shade of emerald green.

McDonnell Douglas DC-10-30 TU-TAM at Zurich. (Marcel Walther)

AIR ALGERIE

Air Algerie was originally formed in 1946 as CGTA, operating non-scheduled flights followed by regular services connecting the French colony with Paris, Marseille and Toulouse in France. The present title was adopted in April 1953 when Compagnie Air Transport was absorbed. Today the state-owned airline flies over a scheduled network which includes over thirty cities in Europe and Africa plus domestic trunk routes.

Twenty-four Boeing jets (eleven 727-200s and thirteen Boeing 737-200s) are supplemented by two flagship Airbus Industrie A310s, used for the primary routes to Europe. A fleet of eighteen Beech 'twins' handles air-taxi work and eighteen Grumman Ag-cats provide platforms for aerial spraying which also comes within Air Algerie's domain; all wear the company's colours, although many have yet to be repainted into the new livery.

Air Algerie unveiled its brand new livery design in mid-1982, replacing the traditional orange and white colourscheme which had been worn for many years. The triple cheatline of two red stripes separated by a green, commences at the black nose radome and flows along the fuselage; the red and green ending at the rear with the top red gracefully sweeping up in line with the fin's leading edge. An all-white tail displays the company's logo, now in red, which is said to represent the Arabic equivalent of the company's two letter code, 'AH', and matching fuselage lettering reads 'Air Algerie' in English followed by Arabic on both sides; the Algerian flag is positioned alongside the forward passenger doors.

Airbus Industrie A310-203 7T-VJC at Paris-Orly. (Philippe Petit)

AIR ATLANTIS

During 1985 the Portuguese national airline TAP Air Portugal, decided that its passenger charter services could be more effectively operated and expanded by the formation of a wholly owned charter subsidiary, to be known as Air Atlantis. With its main base at Faro on the south coast, Air Atlantis commenced operations during the spring of 1985, using three Boeing jets transferred from the parent company, two Boeing 737s and Boeing 707.

The livery worn by all three aircraft retains the red and green cheatline of the parent company, but now extended to the rear of the fuselage instead of sweeping up onto the tail. The fin has been repainted white overall to display the newly-designed 'A' logo in two strokes of red and green respectively. An ingenious titling arrangement replaces the first 'A' of 'Air' and 'Atlantis' with the company logo, the first in green and black and the second in red and black.

Boeing 707-382B CS-TBA at Manchester. (George Ditchfield)

AIR BRIDGE CARRIERS

Since its formation in November 1972, Air Bridge Carriers, or ABC as it was previously known, has offered ad-hoc and contract freight charters from the Midlands to points in Europe, the Middle East, Far East and Africa. Scheduled cargo flights are now also operated over various domestic routes on behalf of other companies.

Air Bridge has the distinction of operating the world's largest fleet of Vickers Merchantman freighters, having purchased six of the type from British Airways in the late seventies.

Dramatic colouring successfully modernises the classic lines of the Merchantman with black and red cheatlines sweeping from the nose, along the fuselage and up onto the tail, following the line of the tail web over a white base colour. 'Air Bridge' titles are worn in black lower case lettering behind the cargo door. Note that although the undersides and wings are finished in pale grey, the horizontal tailplane is painted white.

Vickers 953C Merchantman G-APEK at East Midlands Airport. (Richard Vandervord)

AIR CANADA

Air Canada has existed since April 10th 1937 when it was formed as Trans Canada Airlines, with the present title being adopted during 1964. As the international carrier of Canada, the company provides scheduled passenger services to Europe, Asia, the United States and the Caribbean, as well as maintaining extensive domestic trunk routes.

Domestic and regional flights are operated by a vast fleet of Boeing 727-200s and McDonnell Douglas DC-9-30s, recently augmented by new Boeing 767s. High density services use Lockheed TriStars and the long-haul element consists of TriStar 500s, Boeing 747s and extended-range Boeing 767s. A fleet of McDonnell Douglas DC-8-73Fs provides freight capacity.

The current livery has been used since 1977 and features a warm red cheatline, notably more orange than the Canadian flag, and matching fin. The national Maple Leaf of Canada appears reversed out in a stylised form on the tail, and company titles are carried on the forward upper fuselage in warm red. During late 1984 and early 1985, many aircraft in the fleet carried the 'Singapore 85' logo on the tail, advertising the company's important new service.

Boeing 747-233B/SCD C-GAGB at Paris Charles De Gaulle. (Phillipe Petit)

AIR ECOSSE

A proudly Scottish Airline, Air Ecosse commenced operations in July 1977 from its base at Aberdeen's Dyce Airport, as an associate of Fairflight Ltd. of Biggin Hill. Using Aberdeen as its hub, the Air Ecosse scheduled passenger and cargo network now includes Glasgow, Dundee, Edinburgh, East Midlands, Manchester, Carlisle, Isle of Man, Wick and London-Heathrow, with a Teeside-Leeds/Bradford-London/Gatwick service flown on behalf of British Caledonian Commuter; passenger and freight charters are also offered.

The fleet now entirely consists of British-built Shorts 330 and 360 commuters, capable of carrying 30 and 36 passengers respectively.

The fresh white base colour contrasts effectively with the bright red cheatline extending from the nose, along the fuselage and eventually fanning-out to encompass approximately half of the fin, delicately trimmed either side with gold pinstripes. Black lettering appears in lower case to enable a feature to be made of the accent over the 'e' of Ecosse, and the Scottish theme is continued by the appearance of the Scottish flag under the cockpit windows, above the aircraft's Scottish town name.

Shorts 360 G-DASI at Glasgow. (Gerald McLaughlin)

AIR EUROPE

One of Britain's leading holiday airlines, Air Europe provides inclusive-tour charter flights to all major Mediterranean resorts from its base at Gatwick Airport, including Spain, the Canary Islands, Portugal, Italy, Greece, Gibraltar, Malta, Israel and Turkey. Scheduled passenger services were inaugurated during 1985.

The company's fleet consists of three 'state-of-the-art' Boeing 757-236s, with its half dozen Boeing 737s having been phased-out in recent months.

A bright sunshine image, appropriate for a holiday carrier, is portrayed by the warm red, orange and yellow cheatlines, contrasting with the pure-white fuselage and engine finish. 'Air Europe' titles and tail logo appear in black lower-case lettering and the Union Flags carried on the forward upper fuselage.

Boeing 757-236 G-BKRM at Manchester. (George Ditchfield)

AIR FRANCE

The history of the French flag carrier dates back to August 30th 1933 when a company called SCELA purchased the assets of Compagnie Aeropostale. After the war, Societe National Air France was formed, on January 1st 1946, rapidly reconstructing its impressive pre-war route-network and adding services to the Americas. Air France now ranks as one of the world's top five international airlines offering a vast network of scheduled passenger and freight services throughout Europe and to points in America, Africa and Asia, as well as supersonic Concorde flights to New York. Domestic nocturnal mail flights are operated on behalf of the Postal Administration by Aerospatiale Transalls and Fokker Friendships.

The Air France fleet makes use of eighteen indigenous Airbus Industrie A300s for short range high-density routes supplemented by twenty-nine Boeing 737-200s and twelve Boeing 727-200s, eventually to be replaced by twenty-five Airbus Industrie A320s. Long-haul services are flown by thirty-one Boeing 747s and six Airbus Industrie A310s (also used on short-haul), and supersonic Concordes are now used only on Trans-Atlantic flights to New York.

When the new Air France livery was introduced in 1975 it was widely acclaimed as something totally new in airline colourscheme design. The pure white overall fuselage finish is highlighted by blue 'Air France' fuselage titles and a minute sea horse logo in blue and red. The tail fin displays the major splash of colour in the form of blue and red stripes in varying widths.

Airbus Industrie A310 F-GEMD at Paris. (Christian Laugier)

AIR GABON

Air Gabon was formed in 1951 as Compagnie Aeriene Gabonaise to operate local services using Beech and De Havilland twins from a base at Libreville. The title was later changed to Societe Nationale Transgabon and in July 1968, the airline was designated the country's national flag carrier. In 1974, the present name was adopted and Air Gabon now links all major points in Gabon and flies regionally to Kinshasa, Pointe Noire, Douala, Lagos, Lome, Abidjan, Dakar and Malabo. Points served within Europe include Rome, Geneva, Nice, Marseille and Paris.

Four Fokker Fellowships and a Boeing 737 are used on domestic and regional sectors with a Boeing 747 operating all services to Europe; the company's freight division uses two classic Vickers Vanguards for all-cargo flights.

Air Gabon's bright, modern livery begins with a white overall fuselage that surrenders itself to a grey underside strip on the Fokker Fellowships only. This pure finish compliments a patriotic cheatline arrangement composed of the national colours of green, yellow and blue in descending order. Simple 'Air Gabon' titles, in a brighter shade of blue, dominate the upper forward cabin, whilst the company's green stylised parrot motif is displayed proudly on the fin.

Boeing 747-2Q2B F-ODJG at Nice. (Stephane Salandre)

AIR HOLLAND

1985 saw a Dutch newcomer to the European holiday market under the name of Air Holland. Initial destinations were Rhodos, Tel Aviv and Las Palmas, but these are expected to be expanded rapidly as the company gains momentum.

Two Boeing 727-2H3s are used, formerly operated by Air One of St. Louis, Missouri.

Bright shades of warm orange and royal blue colour the cheatlines over a clean white fuselage. The tailfin carries an extension of the blue cheatline running parallel with an orange line to repeat the double 'L' of the word 'Holland' carried on the centre engine and forward upper fuselage. The remainder of the titling appears in royal blue lower case letters.

Boeing 727-2H3 PH-AHB at Manchester. (George Ditchfield)

AIR INDIA

Air India has been the international airline of India for over 35 years, wholly government-owned since 1953. Scheduled passenger and freight flights connect India with cities in Africa, Europe, the Middle East, the Far East, Australia and North America.

Long-haul sectors use Boeing 747-200s, with regional routes operated by Airbus Industrie A300s, soon to be joined by longer range A310s. Pure freight flights are usually flown with leased Douglas DC-8s.

The company's colourscheme is designed to create the image of a traditional Indian palace with each window individually outlined in red, within a red outlined cheatline. Red 'Air India' titles in English are carried on the starboard side and in Hindi script on the port on the A300, but these are usually reversed on the Boeing 747s. The tail fin also carries 'Air India' titles in English and Hindi in opposite langauges to the fuselage titles in all cases.

Airbus Industrie A300B4-203 VT-EHN at Kuala Lumpur. (Martin Hornliman/S.A.P)

AIR INTER

Air Inter is the French domestic airline which provides scheduled passenger services to major cities on the mainland, including Paris, Strasbourg, Lyon, Nice, Marseille, Toulouse, Lourdes/Tarbes, Bordeaux and Nantes, as well as flying to the island of Corsica.

The backbone of today's Air Inter fleet consists of two dozen indigenous jets, namely the Aerospatiale Super Caravelle and the Dassault Mercure plus wide-bodied Airbus Industrie A300s and turbo-prop Fokker Friendships.

The patriotic red, white and blue colourscheme compliments the liveries of both the international airline, Air France, and the charter airline, Air Charter International. The three-tone blue cheatlines run the entire fuselage length with the upper blue line painted at window level. Bold 'Air Inter' fuselage titles are carried with 'Air' in the medium blue and 'Inter' in red. This livery differs little from aircraft to aircraft, apart for the Friendships which display unique cheatlines slanting at 45°.

Dassault Mercure F-BTTC at Paris-Orly. (Marcel Walther)

AIR LANKA

Air Lanka was formed on January 10th 1979 and flies the flag of Sri Lanka on scheduled passenger services to other points in Asia, as well as to Europe from its base at Colombo.

The current fleet includes Boeing 737-200s, Lockheed TriStars and a Boeing 747, with the additional long-range TriStar 500s on long-term lease to British Airways for its South American services.

A bright red windowline runs from the nose and eventually encompasses the entire tail, forming the backdrop for the company's large white Peacock motif. The whole fuselage is finished in a fresh white with black 'Air Lanka' titles, alongside a representation of the Sri Lankan flag. Air Lanka is one of few national carriers not to base its colourscheme on that of the country's flag, although the brown, red, green and yellow would probably not lend itself to a modern airliner.

Boeing 747-238B 4R-ULF at Paris Charles De Gaulle. (Christian Volpati)

AIR MALTA

The tiny Mediterranean island of Malta established its own international airline on April 1st 1973 which commenced services later that year using Hawker Siddeley Tridents chartered from British Airways. Independent operations commenced one year later with the delivery of its own Boeing 720s, and now include scheduled passenger and cargo flights from Luqa to London, Frankfurt, Munich, Hamburg, Amsterdam, Lyon, Paris, Rome, Catania, Zurich, Cairo and Tripoli.

The current Air Malta fleet numbers three advanced Boeing 737-200s purchased new in March 1983, with three older Boeing 720s now used primarily as back-up aircraft.

The Boeing 737s brought with them a new-style livery, similar to the previous original colourscheme but featuring a modern below-window cheatline. The Cross of St. John, bestowed on the island in the middle ages, is an important feature appearing on the tail in white over a combination of red and blue cheatlines. Distinctive fuselage lettering near the forward passenger doors is in two colours, 'Air' in red and 'Malta' in blue, and the belly is finished in highly-polished natural metal.

Boeing 737-2Y5 9H-ABA (Henk Boele)

AIR MAURITIUS

Air Mauritius was formed on June 14th 1967 as a multi-national venture between the Mauritian Government, Rogers & Co., Air France and BOAC, later joined by Air India. Services commenced in August 1972 with a single leased Piper Navajo, flying to Rodrigues, but have since been expanded dramatically. As well as commuter flights linking the capital, Port Louis, with neighbouring islands, scheduled international services are operated to the Comoro Islands, Madagascar, Kenya and South Africa and even as far afield as Europe, flying to London, Rome, Frankfurt and Zurich, plus Bombay in India.

For some years the fleet made use of Twin Otter turboprops for local services and a Boeing 707 leased from British Airways for international flights, but in 1983 two Boeing 707s were purchased from Luxair and these are now operated alongside a leased South African Airways Boeing 747SP which took the company into the wide-bodied era in November 1984.

The fuselage, all white down to wing level, sports an attractive bright red windowline trimmed below with a similarly coloured pinstripe, and bold upper case red 'Air Mauritius' titles alongside the national flag. A bright red Falcon 'hovers' on the tail, within a white band across an otherwise predominantly red fin. The livery worn by the high-wing Twin Otters differs slightly by displaying 'Air Mauritius' titles between the cheatlines which are set wider apart to accommodate them.

Air Mauritius Boeing 747SP 3B-NAG. (Charles Bargibant)

AIR ZIMBABWE

Air Zimbabwe was formed in September 1967 as Air Rhodesia, with the current name adopted after Rhodesia became Zimbabwe in April 1980. Scheduled passenger and freight services link the capital, Harare, with neighbouring countries and Frankfurt, Athens and London in Europe, as well as Perth and Sydney in Australia. Domestic services connect all major cities and several important tourist attractions.

Five Boeing 707-330Bs are employed on long-haul routes, perhaps overdue for replacement by wide-bodied types, and six turboprop Vickers Viscounts fly local and domestic sectors, recently supplemented by a single leased Boeing 737-200.

In early 1984, the sober blue and white livery was exchanged for something altogether more exciting and dynamic. A quadruple cheatline in the green, yellow, red and black flag colours commences at the nose and 'steps' up to the windowline ultimately embracing of the tail fin, below a new star motif in yellow and red. Simple lower case Air Zimbabwe' lettering is displayed alongside a wavering portrayal of the national flag near the forward passenger door.

Boeing 737-2L9 Z-NAL at Copenhagen. (Mikkel Morbech/Danfo)

ALIA

The national flag carrier of the Middle Eastern state of Jordan, was formed in December 1963 to succeed Jordan Airways, which had been operating for only two years. Named Alia, after King Hussein's daughter, a name which also means 'High Flying', the company commenced scheduled passenger operations between several Middle Eastern capitals and twenty years on, services now include destinations in Europe, Asia, the Far East, North Africa and North America.

The fleet is composed of new long-range Lockheed TriStar 500s in the most part, although four Boeing 727-200s are still used on shorter regional routes and a single Boeing 747 flies the primary services.

Several experimental colourschemes were evaluated over a period of months before Royal approval was finally granted, in late 1982, to the livery which is now worn fleetwide. Under a theme of Jordanian Regality, the resulting image represents one of today's most stylish, with its distinctive red lower-fuselage separated from the cream cabin-roof by triple cheatlines coloured in a patriotic black, red and green. The fin displays a central gold crown motif over a red background and above a repeat of the main cheatlines. 'Alia Royal Jordanian' fuselage titles appear in English and Arabic giving precedence to the national language on both sides.

Boeing 747-2D3B JY-AFA at Geneva. (Jean-Luc Altherr)

ALISARDA

Formed in March 1963 as an air-taxi and general charter company, Alisarda now operates scheduled passenger services from its base at Olbia, Sardinia to Cagliari and across the Tyrrhenian Sea to several mainland Italian cities. Internationally, the company flies to Nice, Frankfurt, Stuttgart, Munich, Paris, Geneva and Zurich, as well as offering Europe-wide charter flights on an ad-hoc and contract basis.

Alisarda uses an all-DC-9 fleet comprising three DC-9-51s and two MD-82s, leased, out of season, to National Airlines in the United States.

The livery, introduced in 1974, is devoid of any identifying logos apart from simple bold black 'Alisarda' lettering near the forward passenger door. A white overall fuselage with grey wing roots, is dissected by bright windowlines in red, yellow and blue, which are repeated at the top of the fin, the uppermost half of which is all red. The company is rightly proud of the latest McDonnell Douglas DC-9 variants it operates, displaying the manufacturer's name and type on the all white engine cowlings.

McDonnell Douglas MD-82s at Long Beach prior to delivery. (M. Bertrand)

ALITALIA

The Italian national flag carrier was formed in September 1946 under the name of Aerolinee Italiene Internazionali (Alitalia) in association with BEA, to operate converted war-surplus bombers over a domestic passenger network. In 1948, the first international flights, to Buenos Aires, took place and the present title was adopted in October 1957 when the company was merged with Linee Aeree Italiene. An extensive route system of passenger and freight services connects Italy with major cities in all five continents as well as providing a comprehensive domestic network.

McDonnell Douglas DC-9-32s and MD-82s form the nucleus of the fleet with eight Airbus Industrie A300B4s used on the high-density European routes and Boeing 747s on the long-haul services.

The image, designed by Walter Landor Associates to take Alitalia into the seventies, was widely regarded as the most modern and stylish of its time and still ranks amongst the most attractive. The livery's centrepiece is an ingenious 'A' logo in green with a red centre, which is formed on the tail as a continuation of the simple green windowline and repeated within the black 'Alitalia' fuselage lettering, in black and red. Note the tiny 'Alitalia' titles in gold on the cheatline alongside each passenger door and that the fuselage base colour is white on all aircraft types, with engine cowlings in natural metal apart from the MD-80s where they are painted grey.

Boeing 747-243B I-DEMF. (Michael Steinlein)

ALTAIR

Altair is an Italian charter operator based at Parma in Northern Italy. 70% owned by Pegasus Holidays, Altair flies mostly inclusive-tour charters for its parent company carrying holidaymakers from points in Italy to Greece, Spain, Tunisia and the United Kingdom. An operations base is also maintained at Luton Airport for services to Genoa, Turin, Milan, Venice, Rome, Naples, Rimini, Brindisi, Pisa and Palermo.

Three Aerospatiale Super Caravelles are operated, all of which were purchased in early 1984 from Finnair when the type was retired by them from front line service; two earlier Caravelle IIIs have been withdrawn from use.

All three fleet members now wear the same livery which was applied upon their delivery to Italy, after having been chosen from several prospective designs. Although it is not terribly remarkable, the scheme is functional and distinctive with its twin cheatlines in royal blue and light blue colouring approximately a third of the fuselage width and sweeping up to encompass most of the tail fin. The company's attractive triangular 'A' motif, which had survived two livery changes, was dropped under the new design, and small 'Altair' fuselage titling in blue replaces the impressive orange lettering of the original design and bold red of its successor. Note that the Italian flag is worn very close to the company name, and that dark blue individual aircraft names appear in the lower light blue cheatline.

Aerospatiale Super Caravelle OH-LSF. (Conti Eugenio)

AMERICAN AIRLINES

This vast Texas-based carrier was formed over fifty years ago in May 1934 as the successor to American Airways, itself formed in January 1930 through the merger of several smaller companies. Now the fifth largest passenger airline in the world, American transports some 25 million passengers each year over a scheduled passenger network which extends throughout North and Central America and to the Caribbean and London, England.

With the airline well advanced on its re-equipment programme, the fleet will shortly number over 300 jet aircraft making it one of the largest in the world, standardised on only four types, Boeing 727, 767, Mcdonnell Douglas MD-82 and DC-10.

The present livery, although still one of the world's most modern, was actually adopted in 1969 to take the company into the seventies, but due to the prohibitive cost of repainting such a fleet, is expected to be retained for some years to come. A stunning highly-polished fuselage and tail finish, provides the perfect backdrop for a patriotic triple cheatline in red, white and blue and purposeful 'American' lettering in red, outlined in white, is displayed on the cabin roof. The tail fin hosts the traditional company motif of a blue eagle swooping down between the peaks of the double 'A' initials.

Douglas DC-10 N144AA at Athens. (P. Collet)

AMERICAN TRANS AIR

Indianapolis-based American Trans Air was certificated by the Federal Aviation Administration in March 1981 as a supplemental air carrier, after its formation by Captain George Mikelsons. Charter services are now offered to points throughout the world but particularly within the United States and to Europe.

The all-jet fleet has been expanded considerably over recent months with the purchase of seven Boeing 727-100s and six Lockheed TriStars, releasing the two Douglas DC-10s which are now offered for sale.

An extremely stylish colourscheme features a triple 'straight-through' cheatline in gold, white and blue, separating the grey belly and white cabin roof which displays large 'American Trans Air' titling in dark blue. A cleverly-designed tail motif illustrates a symbolic runway approach using the company's 'ATA' initials in gold and blue, repeated alongside the fuselage titles on the TriStar aircraft only.

TriStar N185AT. (Damiano Gualdoni)

ARAB AIR CARGO

In August 1981 discussions between the Governments of Iraq and Jordan finally came to fruition with the formation of a new joint-venture all-cargo airline, known as Arab Air Cargo. Services commenced on May 1st 1983 and now serve points worldwide from a main base in Amman, Jordan.

The present fleet consists of two pure-freight Boeing 707s, seconded from the Jordanian national carrier, Alia, which notably carry a joint two-letter registration prefix of '4YB' which is unique to this company.

Both national flags are similarly-coloured in red, white, black and green and provide a basis for the carrier's modern image. An all-white fuselage is decorated with a green belly and matching pinstripes but is otherwise clean apart from red 'Arab Air Cargo' titles in English and Arabic. The predominantly-red fin displays an interesting 'box' logo, constructed using the 'AAC' initials in gold, attached to a combined black, white and red flag. Note that both national flags appear at the rear of the fuselage.

Boeing 707-370C 4YB-CAC at Ostend. (M. Vandaele/Commercial Aviation Slides)

ARROW AIR

Based at Miami, Florida, Arrow Air operates scheduled passenger flights connecting New York, Miami, Orlando, Tampa, Los Angeles, Denver, Philadelphia, Boston, Toronto, London, San Juan, Montego Bay, Georgetown and St. Maarte. Cargo services link Miami, New York and San Juan and the company also offers worldwide passenger and freight charters.

The Arrow Air fleet includes Boeing 727s, four-engined McDonnell Douglas DC-8s and wide-bodied McDonnell Douglas DC-10s.

A number of hybrid liveries have been displayed by Arrow Air aircraft in the past, including several actual company identities, although none of these has ever been worn fleet-wide. The latest colourscheme employs the style of the familiar medium blue livery, but now appearing entirely in red. The broad cheatline runs along the fuselage, below the windows, becoming stuttered as it sweeps up onto the fin and terminates in a huge red 'A' initial, encompassing the whole tail from leading to trailing edge. The overall fuselage colour is white and traditionally-styled 'Arrow Air' titles are carried on the forward upper fuselage.

McDonnell Douglas DC-10-10 N905WA at Shannon in June 1985. (Malcolm Nason)

AUSTRIAN AIRLINES

The Austrian national carrier came into being on September 30th 1957, following an agreement to merge two projected companies, Air Austria and Austrian Airways. However, the company's first service did not take place until March 31st 1958 when, using a Vickers Viscount leased from Fred Olsen Air Transport, a flight between Vienna and London was completed. Today, Austrian Airlines maintains a comprehensive network of scheduled services within Europe, and to the Middle East. Its subsidiary, Austrian Air Transport, offers charter and inclusive tour flights to popular holiday destinations in the Mediterranean, Middle East and North Africa.

A modern fleet of McDonnell Douglas MD-80s is employed, with older DC-9-32s and DC-9-51s steadily being phased-out. Furthermore, two Airbus Industrie A310s will be introduced later this decade, bringing wide-bodied status for the first time in the Austrian carrier's history.

The simple, but delicate livery has remained basically unchanged since the company's foundation. The red, white, red fin arrangement proudly underlines its national identity, and is complimented by 'Austrian' titles and the familiar chevron logo in a matching shade of red on the forward cabin. With cheatlines now displaced, the white upper fuselage and bare metal belly does little to compliment the modern image portrayed by its new generation airliners.

McDonnell Douglas DC-9-50 OE-LDL at Salzbourg. (Richard Vandervord)

AVIACO

Aviaco is a major Spanish carrier based in Madrid which offers scheduled domestic passenger services linking Madrid, Barcelona, Gerona, Murcia, Valencia, Zaragoza, Ibiza, San Sebastian, Bilbao, La Coruna, Vigo, Sevilla, Malaga, Pamplona, Badajoz, Jeres Frontera, Reus, Mahon, Santander and Cordola. Inclusive tour charter flights to other parts of Europe are also offered.

The current fleet consists of some ten Fokker Friendships, to be replaced by indigenous Casa 235s, and nearly thirty turbojet McDonnell Douglas DC-9-30s.

A narrow triple windowline in dark blue (upper), light blue (centre) and medium blue (lower) is initiated at the nose radome and extends along the entire fuselage length, fanning out at the rear to encompass part of the tail in dark blue. Stylised 'Aviaco' titles in dark blue are displayed on the white upper fuselage and the 'A' is repeated in the same style but enlarged on the fin in white, below the customary national tail band of Spain. The lower fuselage on the DC-9 is left in natural metal but on the F-27s it's painted white which effectively modernises the appearance.

McDonnell Douglas DC-9-32 EC-CLD at Prestwick. (G. McLaughlin)

AVIOGENEX

The air charter subsidiary of Yugoslavia's General Export, was established in May 1968 and commenced passenger services during the following April. International inclusive tour and ad-hoc charters now fly throughout Europe and the Middle East as well as to several domestic points, from the company's Belgrade base. Cargo flights are also currently operated to North Africa and the Middle East on a contract charter basis.

For some four years the company's fleet consisted purely of Soviet-built, 72-passenger Tupolev Tu-134s, but in early 1983, a requirement for extra capacity was effectively met by the transfer of two larger Boeing 727-200s from the Yugoslavian Government, since joined by a similar ex-Alitalia aircraft.

Apart from the fact that the black 'Aviogenex' titles are worn further forward on the Boeing 727s, both aircraft types are 'dressed' in identical liveries. The conventional windowline in crimson is trimmed by a lower orange pinstripe which separates the white cabin roof from the grey-painted lower fuselage. The plain crimson fin promotes the company's 'AV' motif in white, which is mirrored on the opposite side so that the streaks emanating from the letter 'V' always trail towards the rear.

Boeing 727-2L8 YU-AKD at Amsterdam. (A.J.M. Hofstra)

BALKAN - BULGARIAN AIRLINES

Based in the capital, Sofia, the Bulgarian flag carrier connects this eastern European state with numerous points throughout Europe, Africa and Asia as well as providing a comprehensive domestic route network. The company can trace its history back to June 29th 1947 and was operated from 1948 as a joint Bulgarian-Soviet venture under the name of TABSO but by 1954 it had become wholly Bulgarian-owned.

A vast fleet of Soviet-built airliners is operated including domestic Yakovlev Yak-40s and Antonov An-24s, Antonov An-12 freighters and Mil Mi-8 helicopters, with international services flown by Ilyushin Il-18s, Tupolev Tu-134s and Tu-154s.

Balkan currently employs three livery variations which are divided among its Soviet-orientated fleet. Perhaps the most significant is that portrayed by the flagship Tupolev Tu-154s, the only type to carry 'Balkan' titles in both Bulgarian and English, the latter on the starboard side only. In all cases, cheatlines and titles appear in a warm shade of red. The Bulgarian flag dominates the fin and provides a solid background for the company's neatly-encircled 'winged-star' motif. On most types this appears on the central green portion of the flag, but expands to cover both the green and red portions on the Tu-154s only. The white 'winged-star' motif also plays host to blue 'Balkan' titles, which appear in the language relevant to the fuselage script. All other fleet members, with the exception of the Yakovlev Yak-40s, wear the reduced-motif arrangement described above, with company titles appearing in Bulgarian on both sides. The Yak-40s wear a third variation which accommodates a sweeping red fin splash, accompanied by a smaller representation of the national flag.

Tupolev TU-154 LZ-BTW at Athens. (P. Collet)

BANGLADESH BIMAN

The national airline of Bangladesh was formed in January 1972, shortly after the country obtained its independence from Pakistan. Scheduled passenger services commenced in February of that year and now connect the capital Dhaka with points in Europe, the Middle East and Asia as well as linking several domestic cities.

The modern western-built fleet employs three former Singapore Airlines McDonnell Douglas DC-10-30s on most long-haul and high density routes, supported by five Boeing 707s, whilst three Fokker Friendships and two Fokker Fellowships fly on domestic and regional services.

The introduction of its first wide-bodied equipment in 1983 inspired Bangladesh Airlines to update its livery to reflect that of a modern international flag carrier. Using the national colours of green and red, the company adopted a fashionable white overall finish which effectively modernised the appearance of the ageing Boeing 707s, and provided a stylish new-look for the DC-10s. The original design has since been slightly revised and now includes horizontal fin bands replacing the original vertical cheatline extension. Black titles are carried in English and Bengali on the port and starboard sides respectively, reading 'Bangladesh Airlines' on the forward upper cabin and 'Biman' on the raised engine. The motif, which represents a white stork flying across a setting sun, is displayed centrally on the fin.

McDonnell Douglas DC-10-30 S2-ACP at Athens. (P. Collet)

BRIT AIR

Based at Morlaix-Ploujean, Brit Air has expanded its operation since the inauguration of scheduled services in April 1979, to become the premier French regional airline within northern France. Scheduled passenger services link Morlaix, Quimper and Rennes in Brittany with London, and also fly to London from the Normandy towns of Caen and Le Havre. Other domestic routes connect Rennes, Lyon, Caen and Le Havre and ad-hoc charter and air-taxi flights are also offered.

The Brit Air fleet consists mostly of Fokker Friendships and Embraer Bandeirantes but two new Aerospatiale/Aeritalia ATR-42-200s are on order for delivery in early 1986.

The fashionable 'linear' design in yellow and black features a tail fin entirely covered in pinstriping which emanates from the narrow low-level cheatlines. Under the cockpit windows, the lines are broken to contain the intricate company motif which represents the Brit Air services with three connected triangles as the Brittany points, three diamonds as the Normandy destinations, and an arrow to illustrate services north to London, alongside black 'Brit Air' titles. Note that the 'Brit Air' lettering can have either a capital or lower case 'B' and that the company motif sometimes appears above the cheatlines instead of within them.

Fokker Friendship F-BPNI at Orly. (Christian Volpati)

BRITANNIA AIRWAYS

Britain's premier charter airline, Britannia Airways, flies ad-hoc inclusive tour charters from points in the United Kingdom to over fifty foreign destinations, principally throughout the Mediterranean and to North Africa. The company was formed nearly twenty-five years ago in December 1961 as Euravia (London) Ltd, originally to operate Lockheed Constellations, with the present title being adopted in August 1964 and take-over by the Thomson Organisation taking place the following year.

Britannia's fleet is well standardised and comprises over twenty Boeing 737-200s and four wide-bodied Boeing 767-200s.

Widely-admired within the industry, the stunning new Britannia livery was unveiled during 1983 and represented an innovation in colourscheme design. Deep blue fuselage-length pinstripes begin at the belly and get gradually narrower as they approach the windowline, each trimmed either side in red. The white upper fuselage displays purposeful 'Britannia' lettering in red-outlined blue lettering alongside a representation of Queen Boadicea's helmeted head, and on the tail the famous British warrior-queen is reproduced as a full length motif complete with Union flag shield, above a repetition of the fuselage pinstriping.

Boeing 767-204 G-BKVZ at Manchester. (George Ditchfield)

BRITISH AIR FERRIES - BAF

During January 1963, two established cross-channel airlines, Channel Air Bridge and Silver City Airways, were merged to form British United Air Ferries. The present title was adopted in September 1967 when the 'United' reference was finally dropped, and in October 1971, the company was acquired by Transmeridian Air Cargo. Now owned by Jadepoint Ltd, BAF is extensively engaged in aircraft leasing, owning one of the world's largest fleets of Viscounts, which are currently in great demand. Scheduled freight flights connect Southend with Jersey, Dusseldorf, Belfast, Basle, Zaarbrucken and Cologne and in addition, passenger and freight charters are offered.

Ten Viscount 800s and two Handley Page Heralds are owned by British Air Ferries, but at present, two Viscounts and one Herald are being leased out to other operators.

A bright patriotic livery in red, white and blue, features a midnight blue lower fuselage, inherited from British Airways, blending into the white upper fuselage via pinstripes in blue and red. The simple blue 'BAF' tail logo is underlined by a broadened continuation of the cheatlines and the fuselage title arrangement reads 'British Air Ferries' in red and blue lettering, with the whole livery brought to life by a large Union Flag. Pure-freight Viscounts display 'Freightmaster' titles in blue and red and the high wing Heralds wear their titles in white and red superimposed on the blue lower fuselage.

Viscount 800 G-AOYO at Ostend. (Michele Vandaele)

BRITISH AIRWAYS

The government-owned flag carrier of the United Kingdom was formed on April 1st 1972 through the merger of BOAC and BEA. Scheduled passenger and freight services are operated throughout Britain and to major cities in Europe, the Middle East, Far East, Australia, Africa, North America and South America.

Boeing 737-200s, BAe One Elevens and Boeing 757s, operate most of the domestic and regional services although the Highlands and Islands division also uses BAe 748s. Lockheed Tristars provide additional capacity for more important routes and the-500 version and the Boeing 747s are used on long-haul flights. British Airways is of course one of only two airlines offering supersonic passenger flights, and employs an operational fleet of seven Concordes.

The new British Airways colours were unveiled officially on December 4th 1984, the first major livery change for over a decade. Landor Associates created a new image which retained the former midnight blue lower fuselage for indentification when airborne, and featured a new brilliant red 'Speedwing' running the fuselage length adding a touch of colour. The top half of the fin is now royal blue displaying a pearl grey coat of arms above a quartered Union Flag. The entire upper fuselage is in pearl grey promoting new-style midnight blue 'British Airways' lettering. All members of the fleet wear the same livery except for the Concorde, which must always be painted predominantly white for heat reflection purposes and therefore does not have a blue underside or grey upper fuselage.

Boeing 757-236 G-BIKO at Heathrow Airport. (Chris Green)

BRITISH CALEDONIAN

On November 30th 1970, charter carrier Caledonian Airways took over British United Airways, and after two years of operation under the name of Caledonian/BUA, the company was renamed British Caledonian Airways. Today, BCAL is the second largest British airline, designated as flag carrier on certain routes and flying scheduled passenger services throughout the United Kingdom and to points in Europe, North America, Africa and the Middle and Far East.

The BCAL fleet comprises two Boeing 747s, nine McDonnell Douglas DC-10s and two Airbus Industrie A310s, plus thirteen British Aerospace One Elevens which will be replaced from 1989 by seven advanced Airbus Industrie A320s.

Highlight of the distinctive BCAL livery is the rampant heraldic lion which dominates the entire tail fin in gold on a deep blue background. A dark blue windowline above a similar band in gold, separate the white upper and grey lower fuselage. Black 'British Caledonian' lettering is followed by the Union Flag on both sides of the fuselage, with the coloquial 'BCAL' logo and shield appearing on the engines of the A310s and DC-10s only. A Scottish flavour is maintained through the use of tartan uniforms and aircraft names, alongside small Scottish flags.

Boeing 747 G-BJXN at Paris Orly. (Christian Laugier)

BRITISH ISLAND AIRWAYS - BIA

BIA was originally formed in 1971 and operated under its own name until it was merged into Air UK in January 1980. Two years later, the company was bought-out by Peter Villa and a consortium of Captains to resume operations under its original title. From its base at Gatwick Airport, BIA now flies inclusive tour, contract and ad-hoc charters to Europe, North Africa and the Middle East.

An all-British Aerospace One-Eleven jet fleet is employed operating in various configurations subject to customer specification.

A simple orange windowline, flanked by brown pinstripes, starts at the cockpit windows and continues on to the tail where it underlines the sloping brown 'BIA' logo. The fuselage, white down to wing level with a grey understrip, displays brown 'British Island Airways' titles situated below the cheatline for maximum exposure to boarding passengers. Note that the registration and aircraft name both appear in brown and that the engines are sometimes painted in white and sometimes left in natural metal.

British Aerospace One Eleven G-AYWB. (Richard Vandervord)

BRITISH MIDLAND AIRWAYS

BMA can trace its history back to 1938 when it was originally formed as a flying school under the name of Derby Aviation. Within ten years, commercial charter operations had commenced and by 1953 the company was operating scheduled services; the present title being adopted in 1964. The BMA domestic network is now extensive and includes London, Liverpool, Teeside, Leeds, East Midlands and Birmingham with services also operated to Paris, Amsterdam and Brussels.

The fleet mainstay is now eight McDonnell Douglas DC-9s, most of the Vickers Viscounts having been retired with four Fokker Friendships and two Shorts 360s flying on the secondary commuter routes.

The BMA livery is bright and fresh, especially on the Shorts 360s where the fuselage undersides and wings are finished in white, with thin parallel cheatlines is light and dark blue separated by a narrow strip of white. Dark blue 'British Midland' lettering is located by the front passenger door, and the blue tail fin carries a light blue band containing the white cross and dark blue 'BMA' logo. The large Union Flag flying proudly beneath the cockpit windows on the DC-9s and Friendships is omitted on the Shorts 360s, which operate within the United Kingdom only.

Shorts 360 G-BMAJ at London Heathrow. (Richard Vandervord)

BRYMON AIRWAYS

Brymon Airways operates scheduled passenger services over a route-network centred on Plymouth, including Jersey, Guernsey, Scilly Isles, Bristol, Exeter, Birmingham , Newquay, Aberdeen, Cork and London.

An all Canadian-built fleet includes three four-engined DHC-7s turboprops flying on major routes supported by two smaller Twin Otters.

Twin broad cheatlines in dark blue and bright yellow separate the white upper fuselage from the grey undersides. The yellow line contains superimposed dark blue 'Brymon' lettering and the upper blue windowline is interrupted towards the rear to accommodate dark blue registration letters. An all-yellow tail forms the backdrop for the curious 'BA' motif, in joined lower-case lettering. Engines are neatly coloured to blend with the fuselage livery in white, blue, yellow and grey and the propellors and spinners are smartly finished in black with yellow tips.

de Havilland Canada DHC-7 G-BRYB. (Keith Gaskell)

BUSY BEE

Busy Bee, a subsidiary of the Norwegian Braathens Shipping Company, was formed in 1966 and soon operated its first service, from Oslo to Kristiansand. Known as Air Executive between 1972 and 1980, the company specialises in sub-services for other scheduled carriers as well as contract charters for the Norwegian military and inclusive tour charters from Norway and Sweden.

The present Busy Bee fleet consists of eight Fokker Friendships, augmented by a single Boeing 737-200, but the company has recently embarked on a fleet update programme which will see the delivery of four more Fokker Friendships and four advanced Fokker 50s.

A comic smiling Bee caricature is displayed on the all-white fin in yellow and brown as the livery's centrepiece with a matching windowline splitting the smart all-white fuselage. Note that the cheatline tapers to a point on the high-wing Friendships, but terminates at the cockpit windows on the 737. 'Busy Bee' titles in black appear on the upper forward fuselage, styled so that the tail of the letter 'Y' underlines the importance of the 'conscientious Bee' concept. It is interesting also to note that on the sole F.27-300 'Combi', LN-NPH, the titling appears higher on the port side only so as not to be obscured by the side cargo door when open.

Fokker Friendship LN-SUF at Amsterdam. (A. J. M. Hofstra)

CAAC

Soon to be renamed Air China following the decentralisation of the Chinese airline industry, CAAC is the international flag carrier of the People's Republic, under which since 1949, all airline services had been operated. International services now link points in China with countries in Asia, Africa, Europe and North America on a scheduled and charter basis.

The present fleet combines a large number of Soviet-built aircraft including Antonov An-2s, An-12s, An-24s, Ilyushin Il-14s, Il-18s, Il-62s and Lisunov Li-2s soon to be joined by Tupolev TU-154s, with the very latest offerings from the major western manufacturers such as Boeing 737-200s, Boeing 747s, 747SPs, 767s, Airbus Industrie A310s, Shorts 360s, British Aerospace 146s, and McDonnell Douglas MD-80s. Numerous older western-built jets are still on strength, namely Hawker Siddeley Tridents and Boeing 707s.

CAAC's simple livery is dominated by a vast national flag which appears on the tail with its leading edge always parallel to that of the fin. The white cabin roof and grey painted lower fuselage half are neatly separated by a narrow dark blue windowline trimmed above by a similarly-coloured pin-stripe. Note that on some types the cheatline runs below windowlevel. 'CAAC' initials appear in black Chinese lettering on both sides of the fuselage, with the English equivalent to be found below the company motif only, usually located near the cockpit windows.

Boeing 747SP B-2444 at Zurich. (Antonio Branca)

CAMEROON AIRLINES

In July 1971, the Cameroon Government formed Cameroon Airlines to provide the country with its own independent air links with the outside world following its withdrawal of interests in Air Afrique. Services commenced on November 1st of that year and now link the largest city Douala with the capital Yaounde and points in Europe and Africa as well as a dozen other domestic communities.

The British Aerospace 748s fly short-haul sectors supported by three regional Boeing 737-200s and a Boeing 707 and 747 flagship for the services to Europe.

The livery has two main points of interest, the tail motif which shows an exotic green bird becoming airborne beneath the Cameroon star, encircled in red, and the tropical style 'Cameroon Airlines' titles on the forward upper fuselage in red. The windowline takes its colouring from the national flag, being predominantly red but trimmed above and below in green and yellow respectively, and widens slightly as it progresses along the fuselage, terminating with a ribbon effect.

Boeing 747-2H7B TJ-CAB at Paris. (P. Collet)

CATHAY PACIFIC AIRWAYS

Although privately-owned, by Swire Pacific Ltd and the Hong Kong and Shanghai Bank, Cathay Pacific is recognised as the flag-carrier of the British Crown Colony of Hong Kong. The company was formed in September 1946 to operate war-surplus Douglas DC-3s on regional passenger and cargo charters, with the first scheduled services introduced in 1948, and is now one of the major carriers in the Far East. Some 27 major cities are served on a scheduled basis in the Far East, Middle East, Australasia, North America and Europe.

Only wide-bodied aircraft are now operated, since the sale of the last Boeing 707s, including nine Lockheed TriStars, eight Boeing 747-200s, two Boeing 747-300s and a single pure-freighter 747.

An attractive shade of medium green was chosen to colour the broad, classically-styled, cheatline, which widens at the front and is trimmed below in white. The all-green fin displays two white streamlining bands below a small Union Flag, but is otherwise devoid of company motif, and bold red 'Cathay Pacific' lettering appears alongside the Swire Group's motif on the upper forward fuselage. The pure-freight Boeing 747, VR-HVY can be identified by red 'cargo' titles between the Swire Group flag and the usual lettering, in a similar style.

Boeing 747-267B VR-HIC at Manchester. (George Ditchfield)

CHINA AIRLINES

China Airlines was formed in December 1959 to provide charter flights using two former military Catalina Flying Boats. In 1966, the company become the official flag carrier of the Republic of China and, since that year, has rapidly expanded its international services. Taipei, the capital, is linked with points in Japan, Saudi Arabia, Austria, South Korea, Hong Kong, Thailand, Philippines, Malaysia, Singapore, Indonesia, the Netherlands and the United States. Extensive cargo services are also operated.

The fleet is now almost entirely wide-bodied except for three Boeing 737-281s used on short haul routes, and a single pure-freight Boeing 707. Both Boeing and Airbus types have been selected, with Airbus Industrie A300B4s and Boeing 767s supplementing longer range Boeing 747s and 747SPs.

As with most national carriers, China Airlines' aircraft wear the colours of the flag, red, white and blue in this case, to create a patriotic identity. The simple cheatline design is repeated vertically up the tail which is devoid of company motif and instead displays the Taiwan flag above the registration. Blue fuselage titling reads 'China Airlines' in English followed by its Chinese equivalent on the starboard side and reversed on the port. Note that the registration is also carried on the forward lower fuselage and that the undersides are painted grey on the 737s, 767s and A300s but left in natural metal on other types. The pure-freight aircraft carry large 'Dynasty Cargo' lettering in both languages flanking the company motif which is not included in the usual livery.

Boeing 767-209 B-1836 landing at Hong Kong. (Norbert Heck)

COMPAGNIE AERIENNE DU LANGUEDOC

Based at Albi in the historic province of Languedoc in the south of France, C.A.L. has operated scheduled regional passenger connections since 1976. Daily services link several southern towns with Paris, including Le Puy, Bergerac, Epinol, Angouleme and Perigeux. Routes are also operated from Clermont-Ferrand to Lyon, Bordeaux, Toulouse, Marseille and Nice, between Bergerac and Perigeux and from Angouleme to Lyon. General charter work is also undertaken throughout France and to neighbouring countries.

A fleet of twin turboprop commuter aircraft is maintained ranging from three Aerospatiale Nord 262s to five Swearingen Metro IIs and a single Embraer Bandeirante.

Several livery variations are used but that worn by all of the Swearingen Metros can be considered the standard scheme. Twin cheatlines in red and dark blue dissect the all-white fuselage and extend from nose to tail. The fin displays an attractive company motif of a white stylised aircraft flying into a red sunset over a blue sea, and full 'Compagnie Aerienne du Languedoc' titles appear in blue along the length of the nose. Two of the Nord 262s wear a similar livery but with an all-blue belly, additional 'CAL' lettering in red on the main undercarriage housing and shortened 'Cie Aerienne du Languedoc' titling.

Swearingen Metro II F-GCPG at Geneva. (Jean Luc Altherr)

CONDOR

Condor is the wholly-owned charter subsidiary of the German national airline, Lufthansa. Formed during October 1961 as a result of the merger of two earlier Lufthansa subsidiaries, Deutsche Flugdienst and Condor Luftreederei, the company now offers world-wide passenger and freight charters and inclusive tour flights primarily to the major holiday destinations in the Mediterranean but also to the Canary Islands, East Africa, the Far East and North America.

Several jet airliner types are employed ranging from wide-bodied Airbus Industrie A310s and McDonnell Douglas DC-10s to a fleet of eight Boeing 727-200s and four 737-200s; a single pure-freight McDonnell Douglas DC-8-73 is currently being operated under a lease agreement with sister company, German Cargo.

Condor's latest livery was originally designed with aesthetic practicality in mind though the delivery in early 1985 of the first Airbus Industrie A310s necessitated a change from the previous natural metal fuselage finish to a more distinctive overal pale grey, which is now being adopted fleet-wide. A bright yellow fin adds a welcome touch of colour and displays the stylised company motif of a deep blue encircled 'Condor', repeated under the cockpit windows and on each engine cowling, complimented by bold blue 'Condor' lettering near the forward passenger door.

Airbus Industrie A310-203 D-AICN at Athens. (P. Collet)

CORSE AIR INTERNATIONAL

Corse Air International is a small Corsican airline providing international charter flights throughout Europe, in addition to regular services linking Paris and Malta.

An expanding fleet of all-jet Aerospatiale Caravelle 6Ns is employed, operating from bases at Paris and Ajaccio in Corsica.

The new Corse Air colourscheme, unveiled in mid-1985, promotes a Corsican image at the tail with the French flag carrying a superimposed 'Corsican head' in black with a white headband. Dual red cheatlines extend from front to rear under the windows and are complimented by bold red 'Corse Air International' fuselage titles. Although the fuselage finish is basically white overall as is the current fashion, the extreme lower part is finished in a more practical grey.

Aerospatiale Caravelle 6N F-BVPZ at Paris-Orly in July 1985. (Christian Laugier)

CP AIR

On January 31st 1942, the Canadian Pacific Railway took over a group of ten small Canadian bush airlines and unified them under the name of Canadian Pacific Air Lines Ltd. By 1968, the name had been changed to the more dynamic 'CP Air' and scheduled passenger and freight services now fly on trunk routes within Canada and internationally to the United States, South America, Europe, the Far East and Australia.

Nineteen Boeing 737-217s have recently been joined by the first of ten ordered 737-300s, whilst long haul and high density routes are served by four Boeing 747s and nine McDonnell Douglas DC-10s.

The innovative CP Air colourscheme features a broad red diagonal cheatline which separates the bright orange upper fuselage from the polished natural metal undersides. 'CP Air' titles, the registration and fleet number are all applied in black, as is the 'Canada' lettering which appears alongside the national flag. The fin displays a red and white portrayal of the current Canadian Pacific Railways logo which can loosely be described as a red right angled triangle within a white irregular semi circle carried at the rear of the tail. Note that the nose radomes on all aircraft are painted grey with a black tip. Although the standard livery is worn almost fleet wide, several aircraft are currently displaying large white 'Expo 86' tail lettering, to advertise the forthcoming world trade exposition, and two Boeing 737-300s are carrying a completely different gun metal and off-white CP Air 'Attache' livery.

McDonnell Douglas DC-10-30 C-GCPC at Milan. (Dario Cocco)

CROSSAIR

Crossair was formed on February 14th 1975 as Business Flyers Basel Ltd and adopted the present title some three and a half years later to promote a more international image. Scheduled regional passenger services connect Zurich, Basle and Geneva with Amsterdam, Brussels, Paris, Luxembourg, Frankfurt, Strasbourg, Munich, Innsbruck, Klagenfurt, Berne, Lugano, Nice and Venice. European charter services are also offered.

The Crossair fleet is one of the most modern of its type in Europe, with nine Swearingen Metro IIIs gradually being joined by ten larger SAAB-Fairchild 340s for which the company was a launch customer.

The present livery was introduced with the first SAAB-Fairchild 340 in May 1984, and as with all other Swiss international airlines, features a tail embraced by the national flag of a white cross on a red background. An unusual cheatline arrangement creates a 'streamer' effect with the top line in blue and the lower in black, eventually petering-out in shades of grey. 'Crossair' titles in bright red balance the livery beautifully and are displayed on the upper fuselage which is white overall as are the engines.

SAAB-Fairchild 340 HB-AHB at Lugano-Agno. (Dario Cocco)

CSA CZECHOSLOVAK AIRLINES

CSA can trace its history back to July 1923 with its foundation as Czechoslovenske Statni Aerolinie. Operations began on October 28th between Prague and Bratislava using ex-military A-14 bi-planes and in 1930 the first international services were inaugurated which soon encompassed much of Europe. After a six year suspension of operations during the Second World War, the present CSA was formed on September 15th 1945 through the merger of the pre-war CSA, Ceskoslovenska Letecka Spolecnost and Slovenska Letecka Akciova Spolecnost. CSA currently maintains an extensive scheduled passenger and freight network centred on Prague but embracing cities throughout Europe and points in North America, the Middle East, North Africa and Australasia.

CSA's fleet comprises all Soviet-built aircraft with Tupolev Tu-134s and Ilyushin Il-62s used on most international services, although two ageing Ilyushin Il-18s are still 'on strength'. Out of a fleet of sixteen short-haul Yakovlev Yak-40s, only four are presently operational, the others having been withdrawn from service in recent months.

The centrepiece of this, otherwise unremarkable livery is the prominant 'OK Jet' tail logo which is a reference to the country's international registration prefix and appears below the national flag on the all-red fin. A simple red windowline is trimmed below by a narrower pinstripe and red 'Ceskoslovenske Aerolinie' titling is worn unusually rearward on the upper fuselage, in Czechoslovakian on both sides. The piston-engined Ilyushin Il-18s wear an old-style livery which features a more intricate cheatline and national flag replacing the 'OK Jet' logo on the tail.

Tupolev Tu-134A OK-AFB at London-Heathrow. (Richard Vandervord)

CTA - COMPAGNIE DE TRANSPORT AERIEN

Formed in October 1978 to take over from SATA, CTA offers inclusive tour, ad-hoc and contract charters from its base at Geneva in South Western Switzerland, to points throughout Europe, the Middle East and North Africa. The company's majority shareholder is Swissair with 57% of the capital.

The CTA fleet consists of four Aerospatiale Super Caravelles, mostly acquired from SATA in 1978, and offering customised interiors ranging from executive, with lounge area, settees and tables, to first class with 52 seats and standard class with 97 seats.

The livery is simple but designed to promote the image of Swiss quality, with the top part of the fin entirely embraced by the national flag. A modern cheatline in red, outlined in bright yellow, starts narrow at the black nose radome and widens along the fuselage. The remainder of the fuselage is finished in white down to a bare metal understrip, with passenger doors and emergency exits outlined in red. A black 'CTA' motif appears ahead of the forward passenger door and secondary 'Compagnie de Transport Aerien Geneva' titling is displayed above the windows. Note that the last three letters of the registration are carried on the nose wheel door.

Aerospatiale Caravelle HB-ICN at Geneva. (Jean Luc Altherr)

CUBANA

From humble origins in 1930 flying a single Ford Trimotor, Cubana has expanded to become a major international flag carrier for the island, boasting some of the very latest Soviet airliner types. Scheduled services take in Madrid, Paris, Berlin Schonefeld, Prague, Moscow, Ilha do Sal, Maputo, Luanda, Mexico City, Kingston, Port of Spain, Georgetown, Panama City, Managua, Lima, Barbados and Montreal. An extensive domestic network is maintained and international charters are also regularly flown.

The all-Russian-built fleet ranges from tiny Antonov An-2 biplanes to modern tri-jet Tupolev Tu-154s including Antonov An-24s, An-26s, Ilyushin Il-18s, Il-62s and Yakovlev Yak-40s. A single Ilyushin Il-76 remains the flagship of the cargo fleet.

Cubana's suprisingly modern livery, introduced in 1970, displays a stylised national flag encompassing the entire tail fin, but omitting the 'white star'. An extension of the red forms twin cheatlines which completely separate the white fuselage top from the bottom grey painted undersides. 'Cubana' titles appear in dark blue and are succeeded by the national flag on the forward upper fuselage.

Ilyushin Il-62M CU-T1218 at Orly. (Christian Laugier)

CYPRUS AIRWAYS

The tiny Mediterranean island of Cyprus employs a modern international flag carrier to connect it with the rest of the world. Scheduled passenger and freight services link Larnaca with major cities throughout Europe and the Middle East.

Cyprus Airways' fleet is steadily becoming one of the most up to date in Europe, with Airbus Industrie A310s having replaced Boeing 720s, and A320s scheduled for 1989 delivery to replace Boeing 707s and BAC One-elevens.

The colours chosen for the airline of a sunshine island deserved to be a little brighter but the overall livery is stylish and 'up to the minute'. Twin Royal blue cheatlines originate at the nose and widen as they proceed along the fuselage length, separated by an autumn gold line. The tail is finished in Royal blue, a continuation of the upper cheatline, promoting the company motif in the form of a white winged mountain goat caricature. Royal blue 'Cyprus Airways' lettering in the traditional style appears behind the forward passenger door.

Airbus Industrie A310-203 5B-DAR at Manchester. (George Ditchfield)

DAN AIR LONDON

The ship brokers Davis and Newman Holdings established Dan Air in May 1953 as a logical step into the airline business. Today the company is one of the top UK inclusive-tour charter airlines flying from major British cities to numerous destinations in Europe in addition to its comprehensive domestic route system.

Dan Air's fleet has now standardized on five aircraft types, Boeing 727s and Boeing 737s, including the latest advanced -300 series, plus three British Aerospace products, the BAe 111 and 146 and the twin turboprop BAe 748.

When the old red and black livery was finally dropped with the Comets, Dan Air chose a totally fresh image to take it into the eighties. Blue and red from the national flag colour the dual dart cheatlines which originate at the nose and fan out along the fuselage length ultimately encompassing most of the tail where they promote the traditional compass and penant motif. Black 'Dan Air London' lettering is preceeded by the Union Flag on the upper forward fuselage, on the port side, and follows the lettering on the starboard. It should be noted that although the livery described is worn by most members of the Dan Air fleet, the company is heavily involved in the leasing of aircraft spurning a number of hybrid colourschemes.

Boeing 737-244 G-ILFC of Dan Air (George Ditchfield)

DELTA AIR LINES

Delta, one of several vast US domestic airlines, embraces the entire United States mainland with its scheduled passenger and freight network as well as serving points in Canada, the Caribbean and London and Frankfurt in Europe. The company was originally formed over sixty years ago, in 1924, as a humble crop-dusting concern under the name of Huff Daland Dusters, flying crop-spraying aircraft in Mississippi during the summer months and transferring the whole operation south to Peru for the winter months. A mail service was inaugurated in 1927 between Peru and Ecuador, leading to a name change in 1928 to Delta Air Service, reflecting the company's diversification. The present title was adopted in 1945.

Some 250 jet airliners are operated by Delta ranging from the McDonnell Douglas DC-8s and DC-9s, Boeing 727s, 737s and 757s to the wide-bodied Boeing 767s and Lockheed TriStars used on the high density and long-haul services.

The company name was originally taken from the Mississippi Delta and is illustrated by a large blue and red delta on the fin and on the fuselage behind the cockpit, affectionately known as the 'widget'. The dark blue windowline is separated from the 'Delta' fuselage titling by a full length narrow red pinstripe, and at a point in line with the cockpit windows, subtlely merges with the black extended anti-dazzle panel. Although the lower fuselage is now left in natural metal, a broad band of white follows the contour of the cheatline down to wing level.

Boeing 757-232 N602DL at Atlanta in November 1984. (Jerry Stanick)

DELTA AIR TRANSPORT

DAT commenced air-taxi and charter operations in 1967 using a fleet of Douglas DC-3s and has since expanded to offer scheduled passenger services between Antwerp and Brussels. Routes flown on behalf of other carriers include Antwerp-Amsterdam for NLM and Antwerp-Dusseldorf for Sabena.

Four of the present five Fairchild Hiller FH-227 turboprops arrived during 1977 with the fifth being delivered in 1980, and these are now flown on all services, from their base at Antwerp in northern Belgium.

Stripes in three shades of blue, separated by white, combine to form the broad cheatline which begins at the nose and ultimately sweeps up to encompass most of the tail, interrupted only by a high-visibility 'DAT' logo which takes up most of the forward fuselage, smartly coloured in a continuation of the main stripes. The unusual company motif is superimposed on the tail stripes in all three shades of blue and mirrored on the opposite side so that the point always faces forward. Note that full 'Delta Air Transport' titles do not appear anywhere on the aircraft.

Fairchild-Hiller FH-227B OO-DTE at Milan. (Conti Eugenio)

DLT

DLT is a West German scheduled domestic passenger operator which was formed in October 1974 through the re-organisation of an earlier company, OLT-Ostfriesische Luftransport, and is 26% owned by Lufthansa. From its base at Frankfurt in the centre of the country, DLT services link a number of German cities including Munster/Osnabruck, Saarbrucken, Bayreuth, Hof, Hannover and Nurembourg and a Munster to London-Gatwick route was opened in April 1985. Domestic and regional services are also flown on behalf of Lufthansa.

The present fleet centres on six British Aerospace 748s but these are to be replaced by four new Fokker 50s which have recently been ordered from the manufacturer. A single Twin Otter is also operated and several aircraft are flown on DLT's behalf by other carriers including four Swearingen Metro IIIs by NFD, a Fokker Friendship and Metro II by WDL and a BAe Jetstream 31 by Contactair.

Lufthansa's involvement in the company is patently evident in the simple DLT livery which features the national carrier's dark blue cheatline and plain dark blue tail with the 'DLT' logo reversed-out in white on the fin and in blue beneath the cockpit windows. Note that aircraft operated on behalf of DLT usually wear either a hybrid livery or pure white fuselage without cheatline but complete with standard DLT tail.

British Aerospace 748-2B D-AHSD at Zurich. (Marcel Walther)

ETHIOPIAN AIRLINES

Based in the capital, Addis Ababa, Ethiopian Airlines was founded by decree of Emperor Haile Selassie in December 1945 as a means of upgrading the country's international and domestic airlinks. Today, the company flies to over thirty destinations in Europe, Africa, the Middle East and Asia, and serves a comprehensive domestic network which includes numerous otherwise isolated communities.

The international fleet includes Boeing 707s, 720s, 727-200s and Boeing 767s, with a number of smaller types used on domestic sectors, namely Twin Otters, Buffalos and Douglas DC-3s.

Ethiopian Airlines' colourscheme has the classic flavour of a fifties livery, with its attractive tail motif representing three tail feathers in the national colours of green, yellow and red, and its intricate, similarly coloured, cheatline which begins with a bright red lightning bolt at the cockpit windows. The national Lion is prominently featured rampant on the forward fuselage and red 'Ethiopian' titling is displayed in English and Amharic with the national language appearing nearest the nose on both sides.

Boeing 720-024B ET-AFK at Heathrow. (Richard Vandervord)

EL AL ISRAEL AIRLINES

El Al was formed in November 1948 as the national flag carrier of the new state of Israel, and commenced services the following year using a Douglas DC-4 on routes to Europe. Today, the company's extensive scheduled passenger and freight network includes cities in Europe, the Middle East, Africa and North America.

An all-Boeing jet fleet is employed which comprises six Boeing 707s, two Boeing 737s, eight Boeing 747s and four new Boeing 767s.

The fresh white fuselage is dissected by an unusual windowlevel cheatline arrangement which is coloured bright blue until a point in line with the wing's leading edge, where it becomes dark blue with a diagonal wedge. The upper rear fuselage continues the bright blue colouring extending upward to encompass most of the tail fin which is topped by the Israeli flag. Dual language titling appears on the forward upper fuselage with 'El Al' in black English lettering interspersed with the Hebrew equivalent in gold. All aircraft in the fleet wear a similar livery but it should be noted that on the 747s, the cheatline continues on to the nose radome but on other types it commences with a wedge under the cockpit windows.

Boeing 747-258C 4X-AXD at Zurich. (Marcel Walther)

EGYPTAIR

Egyptair was originally founded over fifty years ago as Misr Airwork, and after many years of operation under the name of United Arab Airlines, adopted the present title on October 10th 1971. The current international scheduled passenger network includes major cities in Europe, the Middle East, Far East and Africa; plus domestic services operated under the name of Misrair.

Long-haul routes are served by wide-bodied Boeing 767s and A300s, supported by Boeing 707s, with Boeing 737s used on domestic and regional flights.

The head of Horus, the omnipotent Falcon-headed god of ancient Egypt is displayed in red and black within a gold disk on the tail fin and repeated on the engines. A broad windowline takes its colour from the Egyptian flag and runs from nose to tail above a narrower line in gold. Black 'Egyptair' titles in English and Arabic, separated by the Egyptian flag, decorate the forward upper fuselage. Boeing 767s display 'an attractive highly-polished lower fuselage but this is left natural metal or grey on other types.

Boeing 767-266ER SU-GAJ at Heathrow. (Richard Vandervord)

EUROPE AERO SERVICE

Europe Aero Service is a leading French passenger charter operator which also flies on behalf of Air France, Air Inter and Air Charter International. The company was formed some twenty years ago as a subsidiary of Societe Aero Sahara and commenced scheduled operations in 1966 with a Perpignan-Palma route.

The present fleet is based on the indigenous Aerospatiale Caravelle with eleven of the type currently in service, supplemented by a single Boeing 727-200

A fashionable and perhaps typically-French livery, features a pure white fuselage and fin decorated by two bold diagonal stripes of bright red on the fuselage over the wing and repeated at the trailing-edge of the fin and on the white engine cowlings. Full-length 'Europe Aero Service' titles in red appear on the upper forward fuselage and the 'EAS' logo is displayed by the cockpit windows only. Note that the emergency exits are highlighted in white to stand out against the red sash. The Caravelles wear a basically similar livery but with natural-metal engine cowlings and a smaller, squarer flash at the top of the fin.

Boeing 727-227 F-GCGQ at Paris-Orly. (Christian Laugier)

FINNAIR

The national flag carrier of Finland can trace its history back to November 1st 1923 when it was formed as Aero OY to connect several domestic points using a Junker F.13 seaplane. Today, the company offers extensive scheduled passenger and freight services to destinations throughout Europe and to North America and the Far East. A comprehensive domestic network links over twenty communities with the capital Helsinki.

Finnair has stayed loyal to McDonnell Douglas for some years now and has recently ordered McDonnell Douglas MD-87s to join MD-82s and MD-83s in replacing earlier DC-9-14s, 15s, 41s and 51s. Three Fokker Friendships are employed on domestic services but are to be replaced in due course by five Aerospatiale/Aeritalia ATR-42s, and four McDonnell Douglas DC-10-30s fly the long-haul routes to North America and the Far East.

The livery, as worn by the MD-82s and MD-83s can be regarded as Finnair's latest but as the first of these aircraft has now been in service for some two years and no attempt to repaint other fleet members has taken place, it was perhaps designed to highlight these new aircraft types of which the company is rightly proud, with the MD-87s also to be so painted. On all types, a royal blue windowline is worn over an all-white (or white upper and grey lower) fuselage with the tail painted to represent the national flag. Traditional 'Finnair' titles appear on the forward upper fuselage, near the main passenger door for high-visibility, and on the MD-82s and MD-83s only, a smart fuselage flash in three shades of blue has been added. Note that the company motif, of a white 'F' in a blue disk, is carried only comparatively discreetly on the nose.

McDonnell Douglas MD-82 OH-LMO at Paris-Charles de Gaulle. (Stephane Salandre)

FLYING TIGERS

Named after the 'Flying Tigers' of the Pacific war, the company was initially formed on June 25th 1945 as National Skyway Freight Corporation and adopted its present title early the following year. Starting with a handfull of war surplus aircraft, Flying Tigers soon established a hard working cargo force, laying the foundations and positively aiming towards its present status of being world's largest all cargo airline. Scheduled Trans-Pacific services were inaugurated in September 1969, and these currently serve Hong Kong, Singapore, Manila, Tokyo, Okinawa, Osaka, Seoul and Taipei. Today, Flying Tigers' international cargo network also reaches out across the Atlantic Ocean to points in Europe and the Middle East. And, in addition to its comprehensive coast to coast domestic network, scheduled all-cargo services are provided to Rio de Janeiro, Manaus, Sao Paulo and Buenos Aires in South America. Charter and contract work is undertaken on behalf of the Military Airlift Command.

An impressive fleet of eighteen Boeing 747 freighters provides long haul capability, with smaller Boeing 727s offering reduced capacity on domestic feeder services across the United States.

Flying Tigers' livery is composed of deep shades of red and blue, over a highly polished natural metal fuselage. Strangely, the company's Tiger's head logo does not feature within its livery, although the application of a blue and red fuselage sash is a fine consolation. The company's identity is boldly portrayed by titling positioned on both fuselage and fin.

Boeing 747-123F/SCD N901PA at Heathrow. (R. Vandervord)

FRED OLSEN

The Norwegian Fred Olsen Shipping Group chose to enter the air transport market in October 1933 with the formation of its own airline which took the parent company's name. A small fleet of turboprop airliners now offers passenger and freight charters and contract work from a base at Oslo in the southern Norway, to points throughout Europe, North Africa and the Middle East.

Four aircraft are presently used, three four-engined Lockheed Electras for pure-freight work and a British Aerospace 748 for passenger charters.

A simple livery variation in mid-1985 had a stunning effect on the overall appearance of the company's classic Lockheed Electra freighters. Although the basic design has been retained in essence, it has been modernised by the lowering of the dark blue cheatline, which now dissects a fresh all-white fuselage, formerly natural metal on the lower half. The traditional 'Fred Olsen' titles in blue have been emboldened and note the point after the name to indicate its shortened form. The established company flag motif is still flown on the tail ahead of a rudder which is coloured in the red, white and blue of the Norwegian flag, and just aft of the cockpit windows. As part of the livery facelift, the black nose radome and anti-dazzle panels are now also colour-coordinated in white.

Lockheed L188 Electra LN-FOG displaying the companys' latest livery. (Chris Mak)

GARUDA INDONESIAN AIRWAYS

The national flag carrier of Indonesia, Garuda was formed on March 31st 1950 to replace its short-lived predecessor, Indonesian Airways, which had been based in Rangoon, Burma during the nation's fight for indepedence. The company now provides vital airlinks between the numerous Indonesian islands as well as offering scheduled services throughout the Far East and to points in the Middle East and Europe.

Seventy-four jet airliners are presently operated by Garuda including thirty-four domestic Fokker Fellowships, nineteen regional McDonnell Douglas DC-9-32s and nine Airbus Industrie A300s, with long haul sectors flown by six McDonnell Douglas DC-10-30s and six Boeing 747-200s.

The brand new Garuda livery was unveiled to the world in September 1985 when a DC-10 was repainted to coincide with the Indonesian President's European visit. Designed by Walter Landor & Associates of San Francisco, the dramatic new image centres on a bird motif, consisting of five stripes to represent the five national ideals, which appears in various shades of light blue and turquoise getting progessively greener from the nose to tail, and is displayed on the all-dark blue fin alongside the new-style 'Garuda Indonesia' titles, also in dark blue. A pure white fuselage finish contrasts smartly with the blue tail and titles, and gives the livery a modern and fashionable feel. Note the Indonesian flag which appears alongside the forward passenger door and the Presidential crest behind the cockpit windows which is not part of the usual livery.

McDonnell Douglas DC-10-30 PK-GIE at Geneva in September 1985. (A. Senziani)

GHANA AIRWAYS

The state-owned national carrier of Ghana, was originally formed in 1958 in partnership with BOAC. The company now provides all-jet services linking this west African country with the regional destinations of Lome, Cotonou, Conakry, Abidjan, Monrovia, Freetown, Banjul and Dakar, in addition to an extensive domestic network and long-haul international flights to London and Rome in Europe.

Two Fokker Fellowships handle all domestic and short-range regional services with a McDonnell Douglas DC-9-51 providing both larger capacity and additional range and a single DC-10 used solely for flights to Europe.

The livery, as adapted for the intercontinental DC-10, is based on the national flag and features a broad cheatline in the colours of the Ghanaian tricolour. The Ghana Airways emblem is carried on the centre engine surmounted by a large representation of the flag and repeated on the other engines. Fuselage titles appear in the black of the national star and are accompanied by a further flag. The Fokker Fellowships and DC-9-51 wear an all-white fuselage finish with just a Ghanaian tail flag and standard fuselage lettering.

McDonnell Douglas DC-10-30 9G-ANA at Schiphol complete with additional 'Caribbean Airways' titles. (Ron Mak)

GULF AIR

Gulf Air was originally formed in March 1950 as Gulf Aviation Co. Ltd by N. Bosworth and a number of Bahrain shareholders and commenced operations on July 5th using Avro Ansons. The present title was adopted in early 1973 and since April 1st 1974 the company has been jointly owned by the Gulf States of Bahrain, Qatar, Oman and the United Arab Emirates. Scheduled passenger services fly to points throughout the Middle East and to Europe and Asia.

Eight Boeing 737-200s are used on the shorter routes with eleven wide-bodied Lockheed TriStars employed on high-density and long-haul routes, alongside a single leased Boeing 747.

Gulf Air's impressive livery employs an all-white fuselage displaying an extended chin flash in the national colours of the involved states, purple, green and red. The top half of the fin is similarly coloured below which appears an intricate golden Falcon motif, alongside suitable gold lettering. Fuselage titling in bold gold letters reads 'Gulf Air' in English and Arabic, with the former given precedence on both sides.

Lockheed TriStar A40-TW at London-Heathrow. (Richard Vandervord)

HAPAG LLOYD

Based at Hanover, Hapag Lloyd was formed during 1972 as the means by which the vast Hapag Lloyd Shipping Group was to move into the airline business. Passenger charters and inclusive tour flights connect West German cities with regional holiday destinations, primarily in Europe.

The fleet is well standardised on three main aircraft types, Boeing 727s, Boeing 737s and wide-bodied Airbus Industrie A300s providing capacity for high density charters.

Hapag Lloyd's image is very much that of the Hapag Lloyd group, with the parent company providing not only the dark blue 'HL' logo, but also the colours of the livery as a whole. Twin dark blue and orange cheatlines are conventionally arranged, dissecting the fuselage which is pure white down to the wing level and grey thereafter. By the forward passenger door is located the company titles in dark blue alongside a similarly coloured motif, which is repeated on the bright orange fin.

Boeing 727-2K5 D-AHLT. (Chris Mak)

HAWAIIAN AIR

Hawaiian Air is primarily involved in providing frequent connections between the islands of Hawaii, but also offers a connection to Los Angeles and has recently commenced contract charters to points in Europe. The company was originally formed in January 1929 as Inter Island Airways using nine passenger Sikorsky S-38s and adopted its present title in October 1941.

The company is presently operating a fleet of six fifty-seat De Havilland Canada DHC-7s for most inter island flights, with two Douglas DC-9-51s and McDonnell Douglas MD-81s used on the trunk routes. A single DC-8-63 and three recently acquired Lockheed L.1011 TriStars fly long-haul charter services.

Landor Associates designed the company livery which is still held as a benchmark by many designers. The 'flavour' of Hawaii is captured by the ingenious tail motif which combines the state flower, a red Hibiscus, with the profile of a typical island girl in purple and magenta. The pure white fuselage promotes twin sweeps of red and magenta and the motif is repeated near the forward passenger door alongside the distinctive 'Hawaiian Air' titles in magenta. Although the jets wear the standard livery described above, the smaller high-winged DHC-7s have the sweeps arranged in a more conventional cheatline form, narrow at the front and widening along the fuselage.

Lockheed TriStar N762BE at Paris Orly. (Christian Laugier)

HEAVYLIFT CARGO AIRLINES

Heavylift Cargo Airlines was formed during 1978 when TAC Heavylift was incorporated as an associate company of Transmeridian Air Cargo, both owned by the Trafalgar House Group. Operations began in March 1980 from a base at Stansted Airport in Essex, and the present title was adopted in September of that year. The company now offers general and outsized cargo services on a contract and ad-hoc basis worldwide.

The present fleet includes four giant Shorts Belfast freighters, the largest specialised commercial cargo aircraft in the world, and the unique Canadair CL-44-0 Guppy.

A massive white 'H' initial dominates the tail, casting a giant blue shadow across the all red fin towards the leading edge on both sides. The cheatline includes a dark blue line at approximately window level, beneath two pinstripes in red and blue, with the whole arrangement interrupted twice by 'Heavylift' titles in blue and red at the front and rear of the aircraft. Note that the base colour of the CL-44-0 Guppy is natural metal overall but the Belfasts are painted grey with a white cabin roof.

Shorts Belfast G-BFYU at Paris Orly. (Christian Laugier)

HISPANIA LINEAS AEREAS

Formed in Spring 1983, Hispania is something of a newcomer to the European holiday charter market, offering inclusive tour flights to the popular resort of Palma on the island of Majorca.

Initial equipment was four Aerospatiale Caravelle 10Rs but the company has since added a leased Boeing 737-200, soon to be joined by a second, and although the Caravelles are comparatively late examples, they are expected to be withdrawn from service in the near future as more 737s arrive.

Hispania has already progressed to its second livery after only two years of operation. The latest image includes a modern wedge cheatline, running below window level which begins in orange and becomes bright yellow approximately one third of the way along the fuselage. Attractively-styled fuselage titles read 'Hispania' in orange with a superimposed white sun casting its rays across the lettering, with this effect repeated over the 'H' initial worn on the bright yellow tail fin.

Boeing 737-2K2 EC-DVN. (Marcel Walther)

HOLIDAY EXPRESS

Formed in March 1974 and known as Hadag Air until the Hadag Shipping Line pulled-out in 1983, Holiday Express now flies scheduled passenger services from its Hamburg base to Rotterdam, Dortmund, Paderborn, Zurich, Helgoland and Westerland.

A new fifteen passenger Dornier Do-228-100 is used on the primary routes but single examples of several smaller types are also operated including DHC-6 Twin Otter, Britten Norman Islander, Cessna 340 and Cessna 402.

The colourful Holiday Express livery is unmistakably that of a German airline, with its low-slung cheatline in bands of black, red and yellow over a pure white fuselage finish. Black titling appears near the rear passenger door on the Dornier but below the cheatline towards the front of the Twin Otter, and four black chevrons form the company's tail motif.

Dornier Do.228-100 D-IDOM at Hamburg in October 1984. (Udo Weisse)

IBERIA

The national airline of Spain can trace its history back to July 7th 1940 with its formation as Linhas Aereas de Espana by the Spanish Government and Deutsche Lufthansa, eventually being nationalised on September 30th 1944. The present scheduled passenger and freight network is naturally comprehensive, linking all major Spanish cities with destinations in the Americas, Africa, the Middle East and Europe, as well as domestic flights.

Long-haul flights are served by seven Boeing 747s and eight McDonnell Douglas DC-10s, with regional and domestic services operated by twenty-six McDonnell Douglas DC-9-32s, thirty-one Boeing 727-256s and six wide-bodied Airbus Industrie A300s.

A bright sunshine livery successfully combines the colours of the flag with a clue to the country's holiday attraction. Triple cheatlines in red, orange and yellow commence on the cabin roof behind the cockpit and sweep along the length of the white fuselage as a window line. An ingenious 'IB' tail motif in red and yellow includes a small gold crown in honour of the country's monarchy, and the Iberia logo is carried in white on the fuselage and sometimes also in red on the engines.

Airbus Industrie A300B4 EC-DNQ. (Marcel Walther)

ICELANDAIR

The Icelandic national airline was originally formed on June 3rd 1937 under the name of Flugfelag Akureyar and commenced services using a single Waco floatplane between Akureyri and Reykjavik. Subsequent name changes occurred in 1940 when the title of Flugfelag Islands was adopted followed by the present title in 1956, and in July 1973 the company was merged with Icelandic Airlines. Today's Icelandair connects ten domestic towns and flies from Reykjavik, across the North Atlantic to a number of major cities in Europe and North America, maintaining vital links with the rest of the world.

Four Fokker Friendships are used on domestic routes whilst two Boeing 727s and six, various model, McDonnell Douglas DC-8s fly internationally.

A conventionally-shaped windowline in medium blue is trimmed below by a parallel pinstripe, similarly-coloured. Simple black 'Icelandair' lettering is reproduced on the upper forward fuselage alongside the Icelandic flag but it should be noted that domestic types display alternative 'Flugleidir' titles, the Icelandic equivalent, but an otherwise similar scheme. The company motif, worn on the tail, clearly represents the 'F' initial of Flugleidir on the port side but on the opposite side the image is mirrored.

McDonnell Douglas DC-8-63 TF-FLV at Shannon in April 1985. (Malcolm Nason)

INEX ADRIA

Based at Ljubljana in northern Yugoslavia, Inex Adria is a major charter airline which was formed in 1968 as the successor to Adria Aviopromet founded some seven years earlier. Charter and inclusive tour flights link Ljubljana and Dubrovnik with major cities throughout Europe, although a number of scheduled domestic passenger services are also operated.

The company's modern western-built fleet includes four McDonnell Douglas DC-9-30s, two DC-9-51s, four new MD-82s and two 50-seat DHC-7 Commuters. Inex Adria will also be the proud owners of five Airbus Industrie A320s from 1988.

Perhaps Inex Adria will take the opportunity to introduce a new livery to coincide with the delivery of the A320s. The present image is now somewhat dated with its cheatline, sub-divided by three narrow blue pinstripes between two broader blue lines, separating the white roof from the silver or grey belly. Blue titles read 'Inex Adria Aviopromet' on the starboard side and 'Inex Adria Airways' on the port with the 'AA' tail motif unchanged since the company's formation. Note that the registration appears twice, on the rear fuselage and, in full, at the top of the tail, and that the high-wing DHC-7s wear their titles below the cheatline.

McDonnell Douglas MD-82 YU-AJZ at Manchester. (George Ditchfield)

INTERFLUG

Interflug, the state-owned airline of East Germany operates an extensive international route network to major cities in both eastern and western Europe, plus Havana, Casablanca, Algiers, Tripoli, Cairo, Lagos, Luanda, Maputo, Khartoum, Addis Ababa, Beirut, Damascus, Dubai, Baghdad, Karachi and Hanoi. The company also provides additional services such as charters, flying school, aerial spraying and survey.

The passenger fleet consists of almost exclusively Soviet-built airliners including Tupolev Tu-134 and Ilyushin Il-62 jets and Ilyushin Il-18s, Antonov An-26s and Czechoslovakian-built Let Turbolets.

A clean but unremarkable colourscheme uses the bright red of the national flag as its basis. The predominantly red tail fin displays the East German flag in a white band, in addition to the company's white 'dart' motif, repeated in red under the cockpit windows. A conventionally arranged red cheatline runs at window level from nose to tail and is surmounted by red upper case 'Interflug' titling.

Ilyushin Il-62M DDR-SBM at Manchester. (George Ditchfield)

IRAN AIR

The national airline of the Islamic Republic of Iran, was formed in 1962 when the Government introduced a rationalisation policy and merged two existing independent companies, Persian Air Services and Iranian Airways company. Services now link Tehran with cities in Europe and Asia, as well as connecting several domestic communities, although operations have been cut back somewhat due to the Iran-Iraq conflict.

The fleet is quite impressive, including six Airbus Industrie A300s, five Boeing 707s, eight Boeing 727s, four Boeing 737s, four Boeing 747SPs and thirteen Boeing 747s (some of which are devoted to pure-freight operations), although no new equipment has been delivered for some time due to trade embargoes.

The overthrow of the Shah brought a small addition to the traditional company livery; the large black 'Iran Air' fuselage titles were reduced in size to allow for small 'The airline of the Islamic Republic of Iran' subtitles and a representation of the new Islamic flag. The conventional blue cheatline arrangement and tail colouring remained unchanged, as did the mythical 'Homma Bird' which has always dominated the fin. Note that the company name also appears on the rear fuselage in Farshi script.

Boeing 747-286B/SCD EP-IAG at Paris. (Christian Laugier)

IRAQI AIRWAYS

The national airline of Iraq was formed as part of Iraqi state railways in December 1945, operating its first service the following month using de Havilland Rapides. International services now serve twenty-one European cities, plus points in the Middle East and Far East Asia. Domestic flights link Baghdad, Mosul and Basra.

The main commercial fleet is comprised of four Boeing jet types, the 707, 727, 737 and 747, but much of the fleet has a military cargo or government VIP role including Antonov An-12s, An-24s, Ilyushin Il-76s, Tupolev Tu-124s, a Boeing 747SP, plus various executive types.

Iraqi Airways pioneered the distinctive 'dolphin style' livery which effectively streamlines the aircraft's appearance. A conventional bright green cheatline is worn at windowlevel but above this, the fuselage roof is coloured in dark green, tapering at the 'waist' and sweeping up to encompass the tail fin. White 'Iraqi Airways' fuselage titling is carried on the starboard side in English and the port in Arabic, with the lettering on the tail reading 'Iraqi' in the opposite language to that on the fuselage, so that both languages are represented on each side. The dark green Iraqi Airways stylised bird motif, believed to be of ancient Mesopatamian origin, appears in a white disk on the fin. It should be noted that although the livery described is worn by all the commercial aircraft, government and military transports usually wear various hybrid finishes in white and grey with green 'Iraqi Airways' titles and logo and more prominent national flag.

Boeing 727-270 YI-AGS taking off from Athens Airport. (Marcel Walther)

JAPAN AIR LINES - JAL

The international airline of Japan was founded in 1951 and has rapidly grown from humble beginnings to the point where today it operates one of the world's largest fleet of wide-bodied aircraft. The company's route network extends throughout Asia and to Europe, Australia, the Middle East and the Americas.

Over fifty Boeing 747s of various models are used on the long-haul flights, complimented by McDonnell Douglas DC-10-40s on regional services. Deliveries of brand new Boeing 767s in both -200 and -300 form are just commencing and these will ultimately replace the remaining DC-8s.

Only two colours are used with the red of the national flag contrasting with black to give a 'clean cut' image. The tail emblem consists of a large rising sun formed by outstretched wings of a red crane with white 'JAL' lettering. Above dual red and black windowlines appear 'Japan Air Lines' titles in black, alongside the Japanese flag, and the whole colourscheme is enhanced by the, usually highly-polished, natural metal undersides.

Boeing 747-346 N212JL at San Francisco. (Scott Meredith)

JAT - YUGOSLAV AIRLINES

JAT was formed by the Yugoslav Government on April 1st 1947 to take-over from the Yugoslav Air Force, the operations of domestic and international passenger services using two Junkers Ju-52s and two Douglas DC-3s. Today, the state-owned carrier flies scheduled services to all major European destinations plus points in North America, the Middle East, Africa, the Far East and Australia. In addition, a comprehensive domestic network is maintained and two separate divisions provide air-taxi and agricultural services.

The American-built fleet consists of some of the latest offerings from the world's two major manufacturers, including four Boeing 737-300s, nine Boeing 727-200s, a few remaining Boeing 707s, thirteen McDonnell Douglas DC-9-32s and two flagship McDonnell Douglas DC-10s.

As with many national airlines, the colours of the flag are widely employed providing the blue and red of the cheatlines. The starboard fuselage features English 'Yugoslav Airlines' titling with 'Jugoslovenski Aerotransport' appearing on the port. The traditional red and white 'JAT' logo has remained unchanged and is displayed prominantly on the mainly blue fin. A sparkling new livery was introduced during August 1985 to coincide with the delivery of the first Boeing 737-300, featuring a highly polished natural metal fuselage and a more modern, below-window cheatline arrangement.

Boeing 737-3H9 YU-ANF on delivery through Shannon in August 1985. (Malcolm Nason)

JETAIR

During 1982, a new Munich-based charter airline was born taking the name of Jetair. Passenger services commenced with the receipt of its operating licence in October 1984 and Jetair now flies to various destinations in Europe, the Mediterranean, North Africa and the Middle East on an ad-hoc and inclusive-tour basis.

Initial equipment in the form of an ex-Air Panama Boeing 727-100, was delivered in October 1984 and has since been joined by a sistership with a third on order for delivery in the near future.

The Jetair colourscheme follows the current fashion with its white overall fuselage decorated with colourful highlights, in this case medium blue parallelograms on the forward fuselage and third engine. Black 'Jetair' lettering appears on the tail and the cockpit windows are also outlined in black to add a stylish finishing touch.

Boeing 727-81 D-AJAA (Jean Luc Altherr)

KENYA AIRWAYS

The collapse of the joint venture East African Airways in 1976 persuaded the Kenyan Government to form its own national flag carrier, to be responsible not only for providing a international air link but also to connect several widespread domestic communities. International scheduled services commenced on January 22nd 1977, under the name of Kenya Airways, using Boeing 707s leased from British Midland Airways, and now connect Nairobi with major points in Europe, the Middle East and Africa.

Three Boeing 707s and a Boeing 720 are currently used on all long-haul services but are due to be replaced by two ordered Airbus Industrie A310-300s in due course. Domestic and regional sectors are flown by two turboprop Fokker Friendships and a McDonnell Douglas DC-9-32.

The triple cheatline, taking its colours from the black, red and green of the national flag, runs along the fuselage length, with the red central windowline extended at the front to reach the cockpit windows. Simple black 'Kenya Airways' titling is worn on the cabin roof and the white tail displays a specially-designed 'KA' motif in red within a black outline disk.

Boeing 707-351B 5Y-BBJ. (Christian Volpati)

KLM ROYAL DUTCH AIRLINES

KLM has the distinction of being the oldest operating airline in the world, able to trace its history back to October 7th 1919. As the national airline of the Netherlands, KLM flies extensive scheduled passenger and freight services linking Amsterdam and Rotterdam with 74 countries worldwide.

Eighteen McDonnell Douglas DC-9-30s comprise the short-haul element of the fleet with large capacity and long haul services operated by ten Airbus Industrie A310s, six McDonnell Douglas DC-10s and eighteen Boeing 747s including both -200 and -300 stretched upper deck variants.

The two values of blue appearing in today's KLM livery have been used for over thirty years in various forms. A deep blue windowline is flanked by a bold white stripe below, and an all-light blue cabin roof above, displaying reversed out white registration and fuselage logo, the latter appearing in a comparatively small form. The fin is all white promoting the company logo which consists of dark blue 'KLM' letters topped by a light blue stylised crown, to emphasise the 'Royal' Dutch Airlines.

Boeing 747-306 N1295E. (A.J.M. Hofstra)

KOREAN AIR

Formed in June 1962 to succeed Korean National Airlines as the South Korean flag-carrier, Korean Air flies scheduled passenger and freight services over an extensive international and domestic network which includes points in the Far East, United States, Europe and the Middle East.

The large modern fleet comprises Airbus Industrie A300s, Boeing 707s and 727s, plus MD-82s on order. Long-haul services are flown by Boeing 747s, 747SPs and McDonnell Douglas DC-10s and domestic flights use Fokker Friendships and Fellowships.

The stunning new Korean Air image was unveiled in early 1984 to replace the previous red, white and blue 'Korean Air Lines' scheme which dated back to the sixties. In an unusual step for a major carrier, it was decided not only to change the livery design, but also to adopt a completely new company motif and more dynamic title all in one move. A pale shade of blue colours the entire upper fuselage half, representing the sky, below which runs an elegant silver cheatline, with the undersides in pale grey. The company logo, known as the 'Taeguk' combining the red and blue of heaven and earth, with white added to represent the 'endless strength of progress', appears on the tail fin and forms the letter 'O' within the blue 'Korean Air' fuselage titles.

Airbus Industrie A300 HL7426 at Osaka in August 1984. (K. Murai)

KUWAIT AIRWAYS

Kuwait Airways was formed as a private company in 1953 by a group of local businessmen as Kuwait National Airways, to operate Douglas DC-3s between Kuwait and Beirut, under the management of BOAC. After adopting the present title in June 1958, the company became the wholly Government-owned national flag carrier in June 1963 and now flies scheduled passenger and freight services linking this modern oil-rich state with major cities in Europe, the United States, Africa, the Middle East and Far East.

The Kuwait Airways fleet includes some of the most modern western-built airliners with Airbus Industrie A300s and Boeing 727-200s flying the regional routes, soon to be joined by three ordered Boeing 767s, and Boeing 747s and Airbus Industrie A310s are on the long-haul services, with a number of executive jets used for VIP flights.

An attractive shade of ocean blue was chosen in preference to the red, white, green and black of the national flag, and colours the broad windowline and tail band, trimmed either side in black in both cases, the latter containing the company's stylised bird logo. Dual language titling reads 'Kuwait Airways' in blue, giving precedence to the Arabic version on the starboard side and English on the port, with tail lettering in separate languages on either side.

Airbus Industrie A310 9K-AHB at Paris-Orly. (P. Collet)

LINJEFLYG

Linjeflyg has provided extensive scheduled domestic passenger services throughout Sweden since its formation on April 2nd 1957 when it took over from Airtaco AB. Over twenty communities are connected by Linjeflyg jets and chartered Swedair Saab-Fairchild SF-340s and, in addition, Europe-wide charter services are also offered.

The present fleet numbers sixteen Fokker F-28 Fellowships in series -1000 and series -4000 versions, with two more on order for March 1986 delivery, and the company is also a likely customer for the new Fokker 100.

During 1982, Linjeflyg gave its traditional livery a facelift; the light and dark blue cheatlines were re-styled, tapered to a point at both ends and lowered to below the window lines, over a now all-white fuselage apart from a silver understrip. Dark blue 'Linjeflyg' titles still decorate the forward upper fuselage and the 'LIN' tail motif is retained, but the engines are now painted dark blue instead of the previous light blue finish.

Fokker F.28-4000 Fellowship SE-DGP. (Wolfgang Hut)

LOGANAIR

Loganair was formed in February 1962, but since December 1983, has been a subsidiary of British Midland Airways. Billing itself as 'Scotland's Airline', the company operates a comprehensive domestic commuter network centred on Glasgow and Edinburgh and taking in points throughout Scotland, England and Northern Ireland.

The Shorts 360s are flown on the higher-density routes with Britten-Norman Islanders and Twin Otters operating other services, the latter being particularly well suited to some of the short runways of the smaller island airstrips.

The stylish Loganair livery, as worn by the Shorts 360s, is dominated by an attractive bright red windowline which starts at the nose, sweeps along the fuselage, and ultimatley embraces the tail fin, trimmed below by a narrower black line. The white base colour displays 'Loganair' titles in red and 'Scotland's Airline' subtitles in smaller black lettering on the lower forward fuselage. Note that the livery is adapted to fit the Twin Otters and Islanders differing mainly through the use of a white tail with red motif, which appears in white on the all red tail of the Shorts 360s.

Shorts 360 G-BKMX at Manchester. (Simon Wills)

LOT POLISH AIRLINES

The national airline of Poland was formed in January 1929 by the Polish Government in order to rationalise the country's airline industry through the merger of the two private companies, Aerolot and Aero. Domestic and international scheduled services were offered for over ten years until the Second World War forced a cessation of operations until March 1945 and today's route network connects a dozen domestic towns and provides an international link with all major cities in Europe and to points in North America, North Africa, the Middle East, the Far East and Australia.

LOT operates only Soviet-built aircraft including sixteen Antonov An-24s and nine Ilyushin Il-18s used mostly on domestic flight plus seven examples each of the Ilyushin Il-62 and Tupolev Tu-134 for international services.

Undeniably the most modern and dynamic livery of all Eastern-bloc airlines, the company's colourscheme is centred on a large blue 'LOT' fuselage logo with, on the port side, the continuation of the 'T's' horizontal stroke forming the straight blue windowline. The logo is handed on the starboard side so that it still reads 'LOT' though the transition is not quite as smooth with the windowline emanating from the letter 'L'. The all-blue fin contains an elongated Polish flag behind the historic company motif of a stylised 'Crane' with blue fuselage lettering appearing in English on the port side and Polish on the starboard. Note that most aircraft are named using the following system; Antonov An-24s after Polish rivers, Ilyushin Il-18s after famous battles involving Poles and jets after famous Polish people.

Ilyushin Il-18 SP-LSH. (Marcel Walther)

LTS - LUFTRANSPORT

LTS was formed during June 1984 as an associate company of Dusseldorf-based LTU. Holiday charter flights are operated from Munich and other points in southern Germany to tourist destinations throughout the Mediterranean.

Two brand new Boeing 757-2G5s were delivered in May 1984 and February 1985, the first in Europe outside of the United Kingdom.

The LTS livery is very distinctive, although it does not use the normal bright colours of a holiday airline.

An orthodox dark blue windowline runs from the cockpit windows to the extreme rear of the fuselage, which is finished in white either side. An attractive shade of light blue colours the lower third of the fuselage and the entire fin, part from a tiny German flag. Simple white 'LTS' logos appear on the tail and lower forward fuselage, and the engines are finished in a pale grey.

Boeing 757-2G5 D-AMUR at Las Palmas. (Dario Cocco)

LTU LUFTRANSPORT-UTERNEHMEN

Originally founded thirty years ago, as Lufttransport union, LTU adopted its present title the following year to avoid confusion with an existing company. Passenger charter flights commenced in the same year using a fleet of Vickers Vikings and ten years later the company briefly flirted with the scheduled market, offering services from Dusseldorf to other German cities. Today LTU concentrates completely on passenger Inclusive Tour and general charters, mostly to holiday destinations in Europe but also to Asia, Africa, South America and North America.

The fleet has been standardised on wide-bodied Lockheed Tristars and includes six series - 1 aircraft and two long range series - 500s.

The LTU Tristars are painted in a refreshing bright orange, which colours the cabin roof down to wing-level and encompasses the entire tail fin. All other detail is in a contrasting white including the broad cheatline, registration, centre engine and simple white 'LTU' tail logo, repeated behind the cockpit windows in orange. The lower fuselage half is left in natural metal apart from a grey painted area at the wing root and nose radome.

Lockheed L-1011-1 Tristar D-AERI at Athens. (P. Collet)

LUFTHANSA

The national flag carrier of West Germany operates a vast route network of scheduled passenger and freight services. Over 120 destinations are served within 71 countries on all five continents.

Numerically, the fleet mainstay is the 'evergreen' Boeing 737-200 which is used on both domestic and regional flights; the larger Boeing 727-200s are to be replaced from 1989 by new Airbus Industrie A320s. Three wide-bodied types are employed, Airbus Industrie A310s, Boeing 747s and McDonnell Douglas DC-10s.

Lufthansa continues to stay with its traditional dark blue and yellow livery, which is unchanged for some fifteen years although a number of experimental variations have been tried. The dark blue 'flying crane' logo is proudly displayed on the all blue tail within a yellow disk, and repeated under the cockpit windows and on each engine in blue outline. The dark blue cheatline invariably runs at window level surmounted by similarly coloured 'Lufthansa' titles. Most types in the fleet sport natural metal undersides, apart from the Airbus which has a grey painted belly.

Airbus Industrie A310 D-AICF. (M. Steinlein)

MAERSK AIR

Maersk Air is a Danish charter company offering services world-wide from its base at Copenhagen. In addition, Maersk operates a domestic scheduled passenger service on behalf of the Danish airline, Dan Air, to Odense, Esbjerg, Billund, Skrydstrup, Rowne and Thisted.

Boeing 737-200s and 737-300s handle the charter flying primarily but are also used to some extent on the scheduled services alongside turboprop DHC-7s. In addition, a helicopter fleet is employed mostly for off-shore oil support contracts.

The colourscheme is an original concept employing an overall base colour of light blue. Twin chealtines in medium and dark blue are trimmed in white, as are the passenger doors, and the white seven pointed star motif is also boxed in white. Solid white 'Maersk' titles are carried on the upper fuselage. The Boeing 737-300 engines are painted grey with a small Maersk motif, but the 737-200s have natural metal engines.

Boeing 737-3L9 OY-MMK at Copenhagen in June 1985. (Flemming Lovenvig)

MALAYSIAN AIRLINE SYSTEM

In April 1971, Malaysian Airline System was formed by the Malaysian Government to succeed the joint venture company, Malaysia Singapore Airlines, after this accord was terminated. Services began on October 1st 1972 over a vast domestic network as well as scheduled passenger operations to Europe, the Middle East, Australia and the Far East. Long-haul flights use Boeing 747s and McDonnell Douglas DC-10s, regional destinations are served by Boeing 737s and Airbus Industrie A300s, and short domestic hops use turbo-prop Twin Otters and Fokker Friendships.

Red and white stripes of the national flag are reproduced as twin bold cheatlines separated by a narrow white window line. The fuselage bottom is painted grey on the Boeing 747s and A300s, natural metal and grey on the DC-10s, natural metal on the Boeing 737s and white on the smaller domestic types.

An all red fin displays a white central disk containing the traditional Kalantan Kite motif which overlooks the all white fuselage top and red lower case 'Malaysian' titles. Two flags appear, preceding the titles on the port side and following them on the starboard; one is the national flag and the other is believed to be of Islamic significance.

Boeing 747-236B 9M-MHI at London-Heathrow Airport. (Richard Vandervord)

MARTINAIR HOLLAND

This major Dutch charter airline has grown from humble beginnings in May 1958 as an aerial advertising and joy-riding company to the point where it now operates as a supplemental air carrier offering worldwide passenger and freight charters from its base at Schiphol Airport.

The all-jet fleet comprises two Airbus Industrie A310s, two McDonnell Douglas MD-82s and four McDonnell Douglas DC-10-30s, plus an executive Cessna Citation.

Martinair's effective colourscheme displays a warm red windowline, which on the MD-82s, doubles-back to form a stylised red 'M' tail logo, but on the A310s and DC-10s, the tail logo and cheatlines are distinctly separate. Black 'Martinair Holland' fuselage titling gives prominence to the company name through the use of a bold typeface, and is repeated on the third engine of the DC-10s. Note that the lower fuselage is painted grey on the A310s but left in natural-metal on other aircraft of the fleet.

Airbus Industrie A310 PH-MCA at Las Palmas. (Dario Cocco)

MIDDLE EAST AIRLINES - MEA

The national carrier of the trouble-torn state of Lebanon, was formed in May 1945 by Lebanese businessmen and commenced De Havilland Rapide services between Beirut and Nicosia on November 20th, subsequently extended to Baghdad. Since then, the company has greatly expanded its scheduled passenger network helped by a merger with Air Liban in November 1965 and the acquisition of Lebanese International Airlines' traffic rights in 1969. The company is presently owned by Inta Investments (62.5%) and Air France (28.5%) and during the worst of the troubles, is based at Paris. The scheduled passenger network includes points in Europe, Africa, the Middle East and New York in the USA.

MEA uses an ageing fleet of Boeing 707s and 720s whose numbers continue to dwindle due to war action and although three Boeing 747s are owned, they are leased to other operators as the fall in traffic and insurance risk prevents them from entering the war zone. A Boeing 747 is presently on lease from Guinness Peat Aviation to service the company's Paris-New York route.

Inspiration for the MEA livery was obtained from the national flag, with the Lebanese 'Cedar tree' appearing within a white disk on the all-red fin. An orthodox red windowline is trimmed either side by a red pinstripe, separating the white cabin roof from the natural-metal lower fuselage and simple 'MEA' lettering in red is worn near the forward passenger door. Note that the registration appears in white on the tail and full-length 'Middle East Airlines Air Liban' titles are carried on the rear part of the cheatline.

Boeing 707-323C OD-AHC at Paris. (P. Collet)

NATIONAIR

National Canada is a new Canadian passenger charter airline based at Montreal, which operated its first service in December 1984 with a flight to Port-au-Prince, Haiti. Worldwide charters are now offered and the company regularly flies to points throughout North America and across the Atlantic to Europe.

The fleet consists presently of four McDonnell Douglas DC-8s, two series -52s and two stretched series -61s.

The dramatic company livery is centred on a broad grey windowline which commences behind the cockpit windows and terminates on the red fin in a stylish 'N' logo, reversed on the starboard side. An all-white cabin roof contrasts with the distinctive red underside which displays white reversed-out 'Nationair Canada' titling. Note that although on the DC-8-61s the two words are side-by-side, on the shorter DC-8-52s, the small 'Canada' lettering appears below the main company titles.

McDonnell Douglas DC-8-61 C-GMXQ at Paris-Orly in June 1985. (Denis Fleury)

NIGERIA AIRWAYS

The national airline of the oil rich African country of Nigeria, was formed in 1958 and today links the capital Lagos with other cities throughout Africa, and in Europe, the Middle East and North America. The domestic route map includes Benin, Calabour, Enugu, Jos, Maiduguri, Port Harcourt, Sokoto, Abuja, Yola, Makurdi, Kano, Ilorin and Kaduna.

An advanced fleet of wide-bodied Airbus Industrie A310s and McDonnell Douglas DC-10s is supplemented by a few remaining Boeing 707s, plus regional and domestic Boeing 737s.

The green and white colouring of Nigeria Airways were provided by the national flag, which itself appears on the tail fin superimposed with the green 'flying elephant' company logo. Twin green cheatlines are separated by a narrow white windowline and underline the bold green 'Nigeria Airways' fuselage lettering which appears all in upper case. The lower fuselage is left in natural metal finish, contrasting with the white roof, on all types except the A310, which has a grey belly.

Airbus Industrie A310-221 F-WZEN at Hannover. (Christian Sparr)

NLM CITY HOPPER

NLM is a wholly-owned subsidiary of the Dutch national carrier, KLM, having been formed in 1966 initially to connect five domestic cities. International scheduled passenger services were inaugurated in April 1974, and the company now connects Amsterdam, Rotterdam, Gronigen, Enschede, Eindhoven and Maastricht with points in West Germany, France, Belgium and the United Kingdom, as well as offering Europe-wide charter flights.

The fleet relies on indigenous Fokker Friendships and Fellowships, operating three F.27-200s, one F.27-400 and three F.27-500s, plus four F.28-4000s.

NLM's livery uses the two-tone blue colouring of its parent company but arranged as a conventional cheatline sweeping up to encompass the fin. Comparatively inconspicuous 'NLM City Hopper' titling is worn on the lower dark blue cheatline of the Fellowships and the upper light blue line of the Friendships, with the standard 'City Hopper' logo appearing on the tail. Note that cheatlines are adjusted to fit the two aircraft types, with the dark blue acting as the window line on the F-27s and the light blue painted at window level on the F-28s.

Fokker F.28-4000 Fellowship PH-CHI at Paris Charles De Gaulle. (Christian Volpati)

NORTHWEST ORIENT

Northwest Orient can trace its history back to August 1926 when it was formed under the name of Northwest Airways, to carry mail under a US Post Office contract on the Chicago-St Paul route. The present title was adopted in 1934. The company's route system includes extensive domestic trunk services with connections to all the major US cities, as well as international routes to Far East and European destinations.

The company's fleet comprises over sixty Boeing 727s, currently being replaced by next-generation Boeing 757s, plus wide-bodied Boeing 747s and McDonnell Douglas DC-10-40s, the latter being unique in having Pratt and Whitney engines.

The Northwest Orient livery is simple but distinctive employing a broad white cheatline, dissecting the otherwise natural metal fuselage, which contains a dark blue fore-shortened windowline and bright red 'Northwest Orient' titling. The company motif is a red pointer indicating the direction northwest superimposed on an all red globe, and is carried relatively inconspicuously alongside the titles, but not as expected on the tail which is bright red overall sometimes topped by the national flag. All fleet members wear a similar scheme although the appearance of the natural metal is often enhanced by a high degree of polish and pure-freight 747s have 'Northwest Orient Cargo' titles and are natural metal overall without the white and blue cheatline bands.

Boeing 747-251B N613US landing at Osaka.

OLYMPIC AIRWAYS

Established in January 1957, Olympic Airways is today the state-owned flag carrier of Greece. Scheduled passenger and freight services link Athens with major European capitals, as well as points in North America, Africa, the Middle East, Australia and the Far East. Domestic flights link major points on the mainland with numerous island destinations.

The fleet ranges in size from the wide-bodied Boeing 747s and Airbus Industrie A300s, to the Boeing 707s, 727s and 737s.

The livery uses the most famous of all Greek exports, the Olympic games, as its theme. The six Olympic rings appear in their traditional colours on the dark blue tail fin, which is itself an extension of the narrow windowline. Bold dark blue 'Olympic' titles are carried spaced-out along the forward half of the upper white fuselage behind a pendant of the Greek flag. Fuselage undersides are finished in natural metal on the Boeing 747, 727 and 707 and painted grey on the 737 and A300.

Boeing 747-284B SX-OAA. (Adolfo Tagliabue)

ORION AIRWAYS

Orion Airways is one of the premier UK holiday airlines, originally formed by Horizon Travel in March 1980 to fly passengers on Horizon Holidays. The company now operates to all major European holiday destinations, not only for Horizon, but also on behalf of other tour operators, flying from several airports in the United Kingdom.

A fleet of twin jet Boeing 737s is used including the very latest technology 737-300s, with Orion becoming the first non-US airline to accept delivery.

The bright sunshine livery includes wide triple cheatlines in yellow, orange and burgundy, running the length of the aircraft, and separating the white upper fuselage from the highly-polished natural metal belly. An all-burgundy fin features the company's stylised 'O' motif in orange and 'Orion' titles in black appear behind the forward passenger door. The 737-300's engines are painted grey whilst those of the 737-200s are finished in natural metal.

Boeing 737-3T5 G-BLKB. (Frank De Koster)

PAKISTAN INTERNATIONAL AIRLINES - PIA

The state-owned airline of Pakistan was formed in 1954 to link East Pakistan with West Pakistan, now Bangladesh, using Lockheed Super Constellations. International Scheduled passenger and freight services commenced in 1955, to Cairo and London, and now connect Pakistan with points in Europe, North America, East Africa, the Middle East and Far East in addition to an extensive domestic network.

Long-haul services are flown by Boeing 747s and McDonnell Douglas DC-10s, with Airbus Industrie A300s, Boeing 707s and Boeing 737s used on regional flights and Fokker Friendships serving domestic communities.

The livery obtains its colours from the green and white national flag, enhanced by a regal gold windowline. 'Pakistan International' titles in green alongside their Urdu equivalent in gold, decorate the upper forward fuselage contrasting with the simple white 'PIA' tail logo. The distinctive green lower fuselage reaches down to wing level with a grey painted understrip. Note that the last two letters of the registration are carried in white on the nose of the Boeing 707s only.

McDonnell Douglas DC-10-30 AP-AYM. (A.J.M. Hofstra)

PAN AM

Pan Am was originally founded as early as March 1927 to operate a United States Postal Service contract between Key West in Florida and Havana in Cuba. A period of rapid expansion followed with the route network soon including cities throughout the Caribbean and Central and South America and in due course Trans-Pacific and Trans-Atlantic services were inaugurated using flying boats. Today, Pan Am is one of the world's leading airlines with a route system covering over 90,000 miles incorporating scheduled passenger and freight services to most of the world's capitals, with major bases maintained at New York, Miami, Los Angeles, San Francisco, London, Frankfurt and Tokyo.

The Pan Am fleet includes over 120 jet airliners ranging from Boeing 727s and 737s to the wide-bodied Boeing 747s and 747SPs. Twelve Airbus Industrie A300s and four A310s are now also in service under a re-equipment programme with twelve more A310s and sixteen A320s on order, the latter to replace Boeing 727s.

The latest livery was proposed by Airbus Industrie at the end of 1984 to coincide with the service introduction of the first A300s and after several experimental variations, is now being adopted fleet-wide. Regarded as one of the most effective liveries of today, the new image employs a plain white fuselage down to wing-level, with enormous 'Pan Am' lettering in blue, which is easily readable from the ground even at quite high altitude. It was felt unwise to discard the historic globe logo, so it has been retained on the tail, now encompassing almost the entire fin.

Boeing 747-200 N723PA at Zurich. (Antonio Branca)

PEOPLE EXPRESS

Formed in April 1980, People Express confined its activities to high-frequency, low cost domestic services in the Eastern United States until May 26th 1983, when low-cost, no-frills, trans-Atlantic flights were inaugurated to London-Gatwick from the company's base at Newark International Airport, New Jersey.

The fleet is standardised on only three Boeing jet airliner types, 727s and 737s for domestic operations and 747s for the flights to Europe.

The company's appropriate title is graphically portrayed on the tail by the stylised profiles of two faces, whilst an attractive cream fuselage base colour perfectly complements the intricately-styled triple cheatline in chocolate brown, red and orange. 'People Express' lettering is combined to create a single dynamic company logo in cream reversed-out of the uppermost cheatline.

Boeing 747-143B N602PE. (Richard Vandervord)

PHILIPPINE AIRLINES

Philippine Airlines commenced limited operations on March 15th 1941, only to be interrupted a few months later by the Second World War. Services recommenced on February 14th 1946, using war surplus Douglas DC-3s and have expanded over the last forty years to include points in the Middle East, North America, Asia and Australia, and as far as Europe serving Athens, Zurich, Paris, Rome, Frankfurt, Amsterdam and London.

The company's fleet comprises long-haul Boeing 747s and Douglas DC-10s, regional Airbus Industrie A300s and short range British Aerospace 748s and One-elevens, and Japanese-built Namc YS-11s.

PAL's latest livery, as worn by the Boeing 747s, takes its colours from the crimson and blue national flag and features twin broad cheatlines seperated by a narrow white windowline. The tail-fin is entirely encompassed by a stylised upturned representation of the Philippine flag, although the traditional yellow stars are omitted for the sake of style. The white upper fuselage displays black 'Philippine Airlines' titles alongside the national flag, and the lower fuselage finish is natural metal, often highly polished. The company's A300s wear a similar livery but with a white fuselage bottom, and the DC-10s still wear the old variation incorporating much narrower cheatlines.

Boeing 747-2F6B N741PR at Zurich. (Marcel Walther)

POINT AIR

Point Air is a private French charter airline, owned by Le Point of Mulhouse and based at Lyon-Satolas, which was formed in April 1981. Worldwide inclusive tour charters are flown from both Lyon and Basle-Mulhouse on behalf of the parent company, to such destinations as Delhi, Ouagadougou, Bangui, Montreal and Reunion.

The company's initial Boeing 707 was joined in April 1982 by a larger stretched DC-8-61 and both aircraft are still operated.

Point Air's livery, as worn by the DC-8 flagship, is largely based on that of the aircraft's previous owner, Capitol International, with the distinctive blue and red cheatline arrangement allowed to remain intact, Capitol having moved on to a completely different colourscheme. White 'Point Air' titling appears both at the front and the rear of the fuselage alongside the French flag in both cases and the tail fin is now all-white, displaying the company motif of a small white circle within a larger blue disk. The 707 is in a far simpler finish of a plain blue ex-Pan Am cheatline, matching 'Point Air' fuselage titles and the same tail motif as the DC-8.

McDonnell Douglas DC-8-61 F-GDPS at Stansted. (Dario Cocco)

QANTAS

The oldest airline in the English-speaking world, Qantas was originally formed to operate Australian outback flights within Queensland in November 1920. International services to Singapore commenced in 1934 and by 1947 Qantas was flying to London. There followed a period of rapid expansion and today the nation's flag carrier flies on a scheduled basis to points throughout the world, connecting Australia with Europe, the Middle East, Africa, Asia and North America.

The fleet was, until recently, all-Boeing 747, with some twenty-six of the type in several variants, series 200s, 300s and SPs, but in July 1985, the first of six ordered Boeing 767-238ERs was delivered for which use on some regional services for they are better suited.

The fabulous new livery, a creation of the Lunn Design Group of Sydney, was officially unveiled in June 1985. A 'dynamic and proudly Australian' image is conjoured by the sleek white kangaroo which is contained within an all-red tailfin, continuing around the lower part of the tail fin and trimmed in gold at the leading edge for added elegance and sophistication. The remainder of the fuselage is in pure white, promoting 'Qantas' lettering in black near the forward passenger door. Note that the tail design is repeated on the engines, which are white on the 767s and natural metal on the 747s.

Boeing 767-238ER VH-EAJ at Melbourne in July 1985. (M. Hornlimann/S.A.P.)

QUEBECAIR

Quebecair was formed as a flying school and general charter operator under the unpretentious name of the Rimouski Aviation Syndicate. Following the merger with Gulf Aviation in 1953, the present title was adopted to reflect the company's resulting status. Today Quebecair links over twenty communities in its home state and flies to Toronto (Ontario), Wabush (Newfoundland) and Boston and New York in the United States. Extensive charter flights to Europe, the Caribbean and Mexico are also offered.

Intrastate and regional services are flown by six Boeing 737-200s, and three British Aerospace One Elevens with four turboprop British Aerospace 748s and three Convair 580s used to serve smaller communities; long-range charters employ two recently-acquired McDonnell Douglas DC-8-63s.

The very latest Quebecair livery, as worn by DC-8 C-GQBF and currently being applied to the 737 fleet, includes twin broad cheatlines in complimentary shades of red and blue which flow from the nose and widen slightly at the tail. Recently revised 'Quebecair' titling appears on the fin's leading edge in black and on the lower blue cheatline near the forward passenger door in white. Note that the traditional 'Q' logo worn in white as a feature of previous liveries has now been totally ommitted.

McDonnell Douglas DC-8-63 C-GQBF at Paris-Orly in June 1985. (Denis Fleury)

ROYAL AIR MAROC

Royal Air Maroc was initially known as Compagnie Cherifienne de Transports Aeriens -CGTA, having been formed in June 1953 through the merger of Societe Air Atlas and Air Maroc, and adopted the present title to coincide with the country's independence in 1957. Today, Morocco's flag carrier flies from the capitol, Casablanca, to major cities in Europe, North Africa and the Middle East and across the Atlantic to New York, Montreal and Rio de Janeiro.

Boeing 727s and 737s are used on regional services supplemented by two Boeing 707s and a single example each of the Boeing 747 and 747SP for high density and trans-Atlantic routes.

The livery's centrepiece is displayed on the tail as a green shooting star taken from the national flag, with its bright red tail encircling dynamic 'RAM' lettering. Lower-case "Royal Air Maroc' titles in red adorn the forward upper fuselage, in English on the starboard side and Arabic on the port, above an attractive green, white and red windowline which tapers at both ends. Undersides are painted grey on the 737s and 727s, but are left in natural metal on the Boeing 747. Note that on the 737s, the polished-metal engines are decorated with the company's historic 'winged-star' motif.

Boeing 737-2B6 CN-RML at Paris Orly. (Denis Fleury)

SABENA - BELGIAN WORLD AIRLINES

The Belgian national airline was formed over sixty years ago on May 23rd 1923 to succeed SNETA which had operated route proving services within Africa for three years. Comprehensive scheduled services are now flown throughout Europe and to cities in North America, the Middle East, Asia and Africa.

Sabena's sophisticated all-jet fleet employs Boeing 737-200s for most European routes and Boeing 747s, Douglas DC-10s and new Airbus Industrie A310s for extra-capacity services and long-haul flights.

With the Sabena A310 debut in March 1984, a brand new colourscheme was unveiled which has since been adopted fleet-wide. The new lighter blue cheatline extends along the fuselage length trimmed either side by narrow pinstripes in the same colour. Matching Sabena titles are displayed on the upper fuselage in a new style, but are still followed by the flag and 'Belgian World Airlines' sub titles. The tail fin design remains unaltered, as it has for many years reflecting a traditional stability, with the 'S' disecting a large white disc. Lower fuselage in painted grey in all cases.

Boeing 737-229 OO-SDN. (Charles Bargibant)

SAUDIA

The national airline of the Kingdom of Saudi Arabia, was formed in 1945 and initially operated a fleet of three Douglas DC-3s. Scheduled passenger and freight services now connect the three main Saudi cities, Jeddah, Riyadh and Dhahran, with over sixty points in Europe, North America, Africa, Asia and the Middle East as well as linking over twenty domestic communities.

The modern all-jet fleet includes Boeing 707s, 737s, 747s and 747SPs, Lockheed TriStars and Airbus Industrie A300-600s.

Saudia's livery, essentially unchanged for some years, still appears modern and stylish, featuring a double sub-divided cheatline arrangement in two values of green above two values of blue, separated by a narrow strip of white. The white upper fuselage contrasts with polished natural-metal undersides and displays a complicated title arrangement, in English and Arabic, with 'Saudia' in one language and the secondary 'Saudi Arabian Airlines' titles in the other, reversed on the opposite side. An all-green fin carries the traditional Saudia logo which consists of two swords crossed before a palm tree on a white inverted triangle, above small 'Saudia' lettering in English on the starboard side and Arabic on the port.

Lockheed L1011 Tristar HZ-AHP. (Charles Bargibant)

SCANAIR

Formed over twenty years ago, in June 1965, Scanair is the charter subsidiary of SAS, the Scandinavian National carrier, owned by ABA (Swedish Airlines), DDL (Danish Airlines) and DNL (Norweigian Airlines). Inclusive tour and contract charter services are offered from the three countries, mainly to the popular holiday resorts in the Mediterranean, Canary Islands, West Germany, Austria, France, United Kingdom, Switzerland and the Gambia

Scanair's own fleet currently includes three Airbus Industrie A300B4s and three McDonnell Douglas DC-8-63s, but when additional capacity is needed the company leases Linjeflyg Fokker Fellowships and SAS Douglas DC-8s, DC-9s, DC-10s and Boeing 747s.

The Scanair livery has always reflected the company's close links with SAS and the present scheme is no exception, having been unveiled in 1983 shortly after the new image of the parent company. The pure white fuselage displays a colourful flash, which instead of representing the flags of the participating nations, is painted in sunshine stripes of orange below dark blue 'Scanair' titles in the SAS style. The all-white fin simply displays a vast orange sun and the Danish, Norwegian and Swedish flags appear side by side on the rear fuselage, always in that sequence.

Airbus Industrie A300B4-120 LN-RCA. (Flemming Lovenvig)

SAS - SCANDINAVIAN AIRLINE SYSTEM

In 1946 it was agreed that the overseas services of the national airlines of Sweden, Norway and Denmark would be merged, to be operated by a single new airline known as Scandinavian Airline System. SAS was formed on July 31st 1946 and by October 1st 1950 the three national airlines were fully integrated. The present route system includes cities in Scandinavia, Europe, the Americas, Africa and the Middle and Far East, all served on a scheduled basis.

The vast fleet employs the evergreen McDonnell Douglas DC-9 as its mainstay in several variants, including series 21, 41, 51 and MD-80. Long haul and high density routes are served by five Boeing 747s and six McDonnell Douglas DC-10s, and six Fokker Friendships fly for SAS Commuter.

The stunning new SAS livery was finally given board approval in 1983 in preference to two similar designs, and is now worn fleet wide. A fresh white-overall fuselage finish has, as its highlight, a rhombus in the national colours of the three participating nations, Denmark, Norway and Sweden (reading from the front). Simple 'Scandinavian' titles are in dark blue outlined in gold, as is the 'SAS' tail logo, and the three national flags appear on the rear engines or rear fuselage (reading Denmark, Norway, Sweden from left to right)

McDonnell Douglas DC-9-21 SE-DBR at Dusseldorf. (Michele Vandaele)

SFAIR

Sfair is a French operator based at Bordeaux-Merignac in southwestern France, which was formed in February 1980 and now offers worldwide freight charters specialising in the transportation of livestock, outsize and urgent cargo as well as being instrumental in many relief and aid programmes.

A pure-freight McDonnell Douglas DC-8-55F is operated alongside two Lockheed L-100 Hercules, one of which is leased from the manufacturer pending delivery of its second aircraft.

The full company livery, presently worn only by a single Hercules, features dramatic fuselage stripes in purple, magenta and pink which commence with an arch at the front and are interrupted by black 'SFAIR' lettering which is repeated on the fin behind further leading edge stripes. Note that the lower fuselage half is left in natural metal but that the white of the cabin roof is continued below the cockpit windows to colour the nose radome. The DC-8 wears basic UTA colours, its former owner, with additional black 'SFAIR' titles and the leased Hercules is finished in the cheatline stripes of the Kuwait Air Force for the same reason, with similar titling.

Lockheed L.100-30 Hercules F-GFAR at Paris. (Christian Laugier)

SINGAPORE AIRLINES - SIA

The national airline of Singapore came into being in 1972 with the termination of a six year agreement between Singapore and Malaysia whereby international airline services had been operated by the joint venture, Malaysian-Singapore Airlines. Initial services were inaugurated in October 1972 and the company's route system now includes over forty worldwide destinations served by over four hundred weekly flights.

One of the world's most modern airlines employs four Boeing 757s on the shorter regional sectors with Boeing 747-200s and -300s and Airbus Industrie A310s used on high-density and long-haul routes.

The fresh-white fuselage displays dramatic fore-shortened cheatlines in midnight blue and yellow, below blue upper-case 'Singapore Airlines' titles. A huge stylised yellow bird looks down from the otherwise blue fin and is repeated in miniature on each engine. Note that the 747-300s display distinguishing 'Big Top' lettering on the forward upper fuselage and A310s say '3Ten' by the cockpit windows.

Boeing 747-312 N118KD landing at Osaka.

SIERRA LEONE AIRLINES

In June 1982, the operating agreement between British Caledonian and Sierra Leone Airways was terminated and after negotiations between the Sierra Leone and Jordanian Governments, the new Sierra Leone Airlines was formed under the management of Alia. International services commenced in November 1982 and now include Las Palmas, London, Paris, Lagos, Monrovia and Abidjan in addition to a domestic network linking Kenema, Yengema, Bonth and Gbangbatok.

All services are now flown by two Boeing jets, a 707-323C leased from Alia and a Boeing 720-030B, with the two domestic Britten-Norman Trislanders having recently left the fleet.

The national flag appears alongside dark blue 'Sierra Leone Airlines' titling, and is reflected in the green and blue, below-window cheatlines, over an all-white base colour. A blue triangle on the fin is outlined in white and green and contains a white outlined representation of the company motif, the head of a roaring lion.

Boeing 707-323C JY-AEB at Paris-Orly. (Denis Fleury)

SOUTH AFRICAN AIRWAYS

South African Airways was originally formed in February 1934 to take-over the assets of Union Airways and to operate as a division of South African Railways, using Junkers F13s. Today the company's scheduled route system includes points in Europe, the Far East, Australia, South America and North America in addition to regional services within Africa and an extensive domestic network.

Eighteen Boeing 737-200s and eight Airbus Industrie A300s are used for domestic and regional flights with long-haul and high density routes flown by seven Boeing 747-200s, two extended upper deck Boeing 747-300s and six Boeing 747SPs, two of which are currently leased to other operators.

The South African Airways livery is truly bi-lingual throughout with all titling on the port side in English and the starboard in Afrikaanse even down to the company logo which reads 'SAA' on one side and the Afrikaanse equivalent, 'SAL' on the other. The distinctive bright orange tail fin displays a leaping winged springbok in blue outlined in white, and a dark blue 'straight-through' windowline runs parallel with a narrower line in bright orange below. Highly-polished undersides are a stylish finishing touch, although they are painted grey on the Airbuses.

Boeing 747SP ZS-SPA landing at Athens. (Marcel Walther)

SPACEGRAND AVIATION

Based at Blackpool on England's northwest coastline, Spacegrand Aviation is Lancashire's own airline offering scheduled passenger services across the Irish Sea to the Isle of Man, Belfast and Dublin, as well as passenger and freight charters.

A small fleet of commuter aircraft is operated including three de Havilland Canada Twin Otters and two Shorts 330s, with many services flown in conjunction with Jersey European Airways.

Bright orange and chocolate brown colour the narrow sloping cheatlines of the Twin Otter, eventually embracing almost the entire tail fin. Simple 'Spacegrand' titling in brown-outlined, orange lettering, appears between the cheatlines and the cabin windows and the registration is displayed in brown on the all-white fuselage. Spacegrand Shorts 330s wear a livery development which uses similar colouring but conventionally-styled broad cheatlines trimmed below by a narrow dark brown pinstripe, extended onto the nose and repeated on the tail. Note that titles on the 330 are still in orange, but not outlined in brown, and additional titles appear over the main passenger door.

De Havilland Canada DHC-6 Twin Otter G-BGMD. (Richard Vandervord)

SPANTAX

Spantax was initially formed some twenty-five years ago specifically to provide contract charters in support of oil companies in the Sahara desert. General passenger charters were soon started and these have been extended to the point where the company now offers inclusive tour charters to Spain from many other parts of Europe, with authority to operate ad-hoc charters worldwide.

The fleet has now been standardised on the Boeing 737-200, although four classic Convair 990 Coronados remain in service. Long-haul services are operated by stretched McDonnell Douglas DC-8-61s and a McDonnell Douglas DC-10.

In 1983 Spantax dropped the rather staid livery it had used for many years, in favour of a dramatic new image. The triple cheatlines of light blue, red and dark blue start as a wedge under the cockpit windows and underline the unique dark blue Spantax logo. The tail-fin displays an ingenious motif which successfully combines the 'S' initial in blue, with a bright dayglo orange globe upon which is superimposed a white 'paper dart'. Note that the motif is totally reversed on the starboard side except for the dart which always points forward. Additional motifs are sometimes carried on the engines but are placed so as to match the direction of the tail motif on each side.

Convair Coronado EC-BQR. (Jean-Luc Altherr)

STERLING AIRWAYS

Worldwide passenger charters have been offered by Sterling Airways of Denmark, particularly to the major European holiday destinations, since its foundation in May 1962. Based at Copenhagen's Kastrup Airport, the company is owned by Tjaerborg Reiser A/S, a leading Scandinavian travel company.

From an initial Douglas DC-6B over twenty years ago, the present all-jet fleet now includes three stretched McDonnell Douglas DC-8-63s, three Boeing 727-200s and six Aerospatiale Caravelle 10Bs, plus two executive Aerospatiale Corvettes.

The introduction of Sterling's stylish new livery coincided with the delivery of its first McDonnell Douglas DC-8-63 in February 1984, the main feature being the introduction of a refreshing white fuselage base colour over which runs the new-style twin red cheatlines, terminating on the all-white fin where they are interrupted by a vast red 'S' initial. Black 'Sterling' titles appear well forward on the upper fuselage. Note that the DC-8s usually carry additional 'Skyliner' lettering in white on the lower cheatline but on the Caravelles the sub-titles read 'Sky Jet' in white lettering on the engines and 'Sky Bus' appears on the centre engines of the 727s.

McDonnell Douglas DC-8-63 OY-SBK at Copenhagen. (Mikkel Morbech/Danfo)

SWISSAIR

Swissair has been in operation since March 16th 1931 when it was formed by the merger of Ad Astra Aero and Balair, apart from a break during the second world war. The Swiss flag carrier flies worldwide with scheduled passenger and freight services to Europe, North America, South America, Africa, the Middle East and the Far East.

The fleet consists of McDonnell Douglas DC-8s, DC-9s and MD-80s plus three wide-bodied types, namely Airbus Industrie A310, McDonnell Douglas DC-10 and Boeing 747. Eight new Fokker F100 jets are on order for use on European routes replacing DC-9-32s.

The Swiss flag is emblazoned across the tail boldly stating the carriers national identity, and is complimented by bright red 'Swissair' titles over the white fuselage top. Straight twin cheatlines in brown (upper) and black (lower) extend from nose to tail below window level. The lower fuselage is finished in grey on the A310s but natural metal on all other types, sometimes highly polished.

Airbus Industrie A310-221 HB-IPA at Zurich (Jean Luc Altherr)

SWEDAIR

Stockholm-based Swedair was formed in 1975 as the result of the merger between Svensk Flygtanst AB Swedair and Crownair AB. Scheduled passenger services connect several Scandinavian cities including Gothenburg, Stockholm, Orebro, Borlange, Copenhagen and Karlstad, and in addition, a number of routes are flown on behalf of SAS and Linjeflyg. Other important revenue sources are ad-hoc and contract charters, air-taxi and survey flights and especially target towing for the Swedish armed forces.

The mixed fleet ranges from the new thirty-five seat Saab-Fairchild 340s to Fairchild F-27s and smaller Twin Otters, British Aerospace Jetstream 31, Cessna 404 Titans and Cessna 441 Conquests. Target-towing duties are undertaken by specially-equipped Gates Learjets and Mitsubishi MU-2s and a single Douglas DC-3 is available for survey work.

All Swedair passenger aircraft wear an essentially similar livery which features twin cheatlines in light and dark blue, over an all-white fuselage with the upper line extended to the tail on some types and running 'straight-through' on others. The universally-carried tail logo is a dark blue disk containing 'Swed Air' in white, the latter word sporting a rear wing. Target-tugs wear a high-visibility yellow-overall livery with a dark blue cheatline and standard tail disk.

Saab-Fairchild 340 SE-ISP at Bromma in May 1985. (Svante Nyholm)

SYRIANAIR (SYRIAN ARAB AIRLINES)

Syrianair was formed in October 1961 by the Syrian Government as the country's national airline, to operate both domestic and regional scheduled services. Today, the company's network links this Arab state with points in both western and Eastern Europe, plus the Middle East, Asia and Africa. Domestic flights are flown to Der Ezzar, Aleppo, Latakia and Kamershili.

As with several Middle Eastern airlines, the Syrianair fleet is used for both commercial services and Government VIP and freight flights. Boeing 727s and Tupolev Tu-154s serve on most of the international routes with Boeing 747SPs on long-haul and Aerospatiale Caravelles and Tupolev Tu-134s employed on regional services. Domestic flights use Yakovlev Yak-40s and Antonov An-26s, with Ilyushin Il-76s kept solely for cargo hauls.

Unusually, the national carrier does not take its colours from the country's red, white and black flag, but instead uses a bright Mediterranean blue cheatline over a predominantely white fuselage to compliment the very latest American and Soviet airliner equipment. The titling arrangement on the starboard side has blue 'Syrianair' lettering in Arabic followed by English, reversed on the port side, and the tail fin displays a stylised mystical bird gliding across a blue sun. Note that some types carry Syrian Air titles in two words in black lettering.

Boeing 727-294 YK-AGC at Paris Orly. (Philippe Petit)

TAP AIR PORTUGAL

The Portuguese national carrier was formed on March 14th 1945 and commenced services in September 1946 to Madrid, with Angola and Mozambique added to the route system later. For over thirty years the company was known as Transportes Aereas Portugueses-TAP until in 1979 the decision was taken to adopt a more dynamic and internationally recognisable image. Air Portugal, as the company became, now flies scheduled passenger and cargo services linking the capital, Lisbon with other cities in Europe, North America, South America and Africa.

The Air Portugal fleet numbers eight Boeing 707s, eight Boeing 727s and five Boeing 737s, with five wide-bodied Lockheed L1011 TriStars used on long-haul and high density routes.

The livery chosen to take the company into the eighties is based on a new style 'TAP' tail logo in red and white, whose red 'contrail' trimmed above in green extends along the fuselage from the cockpit windows to form the cheatline (at windowlevel on the TriStar but lower on all other types). Simple black 'Air Portugal' titling is displayed on the upper fuselage, which is white down to the wing level where it becomes polished metal.

Lockheed L-1011-500 TriStar CS-TEE at Paris Orly. (Luc Bereni)

TAROM

The Rumanian national airline was originally formed as a joint venture with the Soviet Government in 1946 under the name of TARS-Transporturi Aeriene Romana Sovietica to succeed the pre-war airline LARES, using a fleet of Lisunov LI-2s. The present title was adopted in 1954 when the company came under the full control of the Rumanian Government, and Tarom now flies scheduled passenger and freight services within Europe and to points in the Middle East, Far East, Africa and the United States, as well as domestically.

The fleet includes both western and eastern built airliners with most passenger services flown by Tupolev Tu-154s, Ilyushin Il-18s and Il-62s, British Aerospace and ROMBAC 111s and Antonov An-24s. Boeing 707s are maintained mainly for government VIP flights although two are freighters to supplement the cargo fleet of Antonov An-26s.

Most of Tarom's jet airliners wear the livery as illustrated with a red encircled bird logo on the tail as its centrepiece and a broad red windowline flanked by narrower red pinstripes either side. However, all the propellor types, and one or two of the Ilyushin Il-62s, wear an earlier variation which promotes the national flag on the all-white tail and relegates the company motif to a point on the fuselage behind the cockpit windows, trailed by a narrower red cheatline with a single red pinstripe below. The titling arrangement is identical on both liveries with large black 'Tarom' lettering flanked by 'Transporturile Aeriene Romane' and Romanian Air Transport' subtitles. Note that although the 'Circle' scheme can be considered to be the latest of the two variations, propellor types are still being delivered in the 'old' livery and no attempt is being made to repaint them.

British Aerospace One Eleven YR-BCN at Zurich (Marcel Walther)

THAI INTERNATIONAL

The flag-carrier of Thailand was established in August 1954 to take over the international routes of Thai Airways, in co-operation with Scandinavian Airline System. Now wholly Government-owned, Thai International connects the capitol, Bangkok, with major cities in Europe, Australia, the United States, Asia and throughout the Far East.

A modern jet fleet includes European Airbus Industrie A300s for regional services and long-haul Boeing 747s and McDonnell Douglas DC-10s, with a few DC-8s still being used but due to be phased-out in the near future.

The beautiful Thai International livery was created in 1975 by leading designers Walter Landor Associates under a brief which called for a reflection of the rich heritage of Thailand in both form and colour. A vast Royal Orchid motif fills the tail fin in shades of magenta, gold and purple and is repeated on the forward fuselage at the head of a broad cheatline which is similarly coloured. Abbreviated 'Thai' lettering appears near the forward passenger door in purple and the national flag is displayed at the top of the tail fin. Note that the registration is colour co-ordinated and is applied in purple towards the rear of the fuselage. Additional 'Rattanakosin Bicentennial 1982' lettering was carried throughout 1982 and 1983 on the 747s and DC-10s only.

Boeing 747-2D7B HS-TGF

TAT - TRANSPORT AERIEN REGIONAL

TAT was formed in 1968, by Michel Marchais, to operate air-taxi and charter services using a small fleet of light aircraft but by 1969 was ready to commence scheduled passenger services on the Tours-Lyon route. Today, TAT is the country's premier regional airline. The company's scheduled domestic passenger network has been expanded over the years with the acquisition of several smaller companies such as Avia Taxi France, Rousseau Aviation, Air Paris, Air Rouergue, Air Alpes and Air Alsace and now encompasses some fifty points throughout France as well as international links with destinations in West Germany, Switzerland and the United Kingdom.

The backbone of the fleet consists of seventeen American-built Fairchild-Hiller FH-227s in addition to nine Fokker Fellowships and these are augmented by smaller turboprop commuters including Beech King Airs, Beech 99s and Twin Otters.

The full company livery, presently worn only by FH-227s, features a unique canary yellow fuselage colour overlaid with a triple cheatline in blue, white, blue, beginning and ending in the white 'TAT' logo, outlined in blue. It should be noted that several of the FH-227s wear hybrid liveries based on the colours of their previous operators with additional TAT logos.

Fairchild-Hiller FH-227B F-GCPY at Zurich. (Marcel Walther)

TRANSAMERICA AIRLINES

Transamerica operates extensive international passenger and freight charters throughout the world and, in addition, is used widely by the US military under contract, flying freight and personnel to destinations in Europe and overseas. Scheduled passenger services are also offered to Europe and link major domestic points.

A fleet of Boeing 747s is used on long-haul flights alongside smaller capacity McDonnell Douglas DC-8-73s. Furthermore, several Lockheed Hercules freighters are employed at the heart of its extensive cargo operation.

The livery is dominated by the established 'T' logo of the Transamerica Corporation, the airline's parent company, which is carried in white on the tail fin. An all white fuselage on the Boeing 747 is dissected by the unusual turquoise windowline, eventually encompassing the tail, surmounted by a light blue and then black band. Black Transamerica titles appear on the forward upper fuselage. Other aircraft in the fleet display a natural metal lower fuselage but the white, worn by the flagship 747s, creates a more modern image.

Boeing 747-271C/SCD N743TV at Heathrow Airport. (Richard Vandervord)

TRANSAVIA HOLLAND

Transavia Holland was formed in 1965 to operate inclusive tour charters from its base at Schiphol Airport, using a fleet of piston-engined Douglas DC-6s. The company is now an all-jet airline flying Dutch holiday makers to traditional destinations throughout Europe and to North Africa, and in addition is involved heavily in leasing aircraft to other carriers.

The present fleet numbers ten Boeing 737-200s, sooned to be joined by two ordered Boeing 737-300s.

An extremely innovative livery has, as its centrepiece, a large black 'T' logo under the cockpit windows which generates two green fuselage lines, light green from the horizontal stroke and dark green from the vertical, in an overall speeding 'T' effect. The black logo is repeated on the tail, outlined in white, and simple black 'Transavia Holland' lettering adorns the upper white fuselage. Although the majority of Transavia's fleet wears the company's livery, the leasing business leads to a number of hybrid colours with 'Transavia Holland' titles.

Boeing 737-2K2 PH-TVS at Las Palmas. (Dario Cocco)

TRANS EUROPEAN AIRWAYS - TEA

Based at Brussels International Airport, TEA offers worldwide passenger charters, particularly inclusive tours to the major European holiday destinations, using an all-jet fleet. The company has been in existence since October 1970 when it was formed by TIFA, a leading Belgian tour operator, to offer inclusive tour charters using an ex-Eastern Airlines Boeing 720.

A single wide-bodied Airbus Industrie A300B1 and two Boeing 707s are operated but the fleet mainstay is the Boeing 737-200, with five currently in service, although aircraft are regularly leased to other operators as an important source of revenue.

High-profile 'TEA' lettering in dark blue is displayed on the forward fuselage as the centrepiece of the company's livery, interrupting the dark blue windowline which sweeps up onto the tail, joined by a lower light blue line originating at a point above the wings. The 'TEA' logo is repeated on the tail in superimposed white lettering and note that the white colouring of the cabin roof is extended down to below the windowline and around the fuselage logo, with the lower fuselage half painted grey.

Boeing 737-2M9 OO-TEL at Athens. (P. Collet)

TRANS MEDITERRANEAN AIRLINES - TMA

TMA can trace its history back to 1953 and the inauguration of cargo flights from Beirut to oil stations in the Arabian Gulf using two Avro York freighters. In 1959, the company was granted a licence to fly scheduled loads and these services now link Beirut with cities throughout the Middle East and to points in Europe.

Seven pure-freight Boeing 707s are operated, but the fleet has been reduced in recent years due to the situation in Lebanon; during the mid-seventies, two Boeing 747s were owned by the company but these were later sold and have not been replaced.

The high-visibility TMA colourscheme features a green overall fuselage finish, to contrast with the sand-coloured scenery of the Middle East, its main sphere of operations. The bright yellow tail displays the company motif of a yellow triangle with superimposed green 'TMA' lettering and black wings, all within a green disk, and is topped by the national flag. The green fuselage is violated only by the registration and 'TMA of Lebanon' titles in yellow, with a small version of the tail motif appearing near the cockpit windows.

Boeing 707-327C OD-AFY at Paris Orly. (Christian Laugier)

TRANS WORLD AIRLINES - TWA

TWA is today one of the world's largest airlines, offering scheduled passenger services over a vast network which includes fifty-five domestic US cities and reaches to Europe, the Middle East and Asia, as well as passenger charters. The company can trace its history back over sixty years to 1925 when Western Air Express successfully bid for a US postal service mail contract over the Salt Lake City-Los Angeles route. In July 1930, Western Air Express merged with Transcontinental Air Transport-Maddux Air Lines and became Trans Continental and Western Air (TWA), and four years after international services were inaugurated in 1946, the present, more appropriate, title was adopted.

Nearly 200 jet airliners are operated including Boeing 727s, McDonnell Douglas DC-9-32s and MD-82s with wide-bodied Boeing 747s, 767s and Lockheed TriStars.

On November 30th 1974, TWA unveiled its new livery to replace the traditional 'twin globe' scheme, which has remained unchanged now for some ten years apart from the Trans World titling which now appears in solid red, replacing the previous red outline. Thin warm red cheatlines commence at the nose under the black anti-dazle panels and proceed along the pure-white fuselage below the windows, widening as they go and ultimately wrapping around under the rear fuselage. The fin displays the white 'TWA' logo reversed out of the red centre section which varies in shape from type to type. Note that the US flag appears at the top of the fin on most types, but on those with a T-tail it is featured alongside the registration.

Boeing 727-231 N54338 at Athens. (Philippe Collet)

TUNIS AIR

With extensive French interests in Tunisia, Air France was naturally instrumental in forming the country's national airline, Tunis Air, which was founded in 1948 as a division of the French airline but with the Tunisian Government and various private interests involved; it is now owned 51% by the government and 49% by Air France. Scheduled services link the three main cities, Tunis, Djerba and Monastir, with twenty-four European destinations as well as other North African and Gulf states.

The fleet comprises five Boeing 737-200s, eight longer range Boeing 727-200s and one Airbus Industrie A300, used on high density flights.

Twin broad red cheatlines run along the fuselage length from nose to tail, separating the white roof from the grey belly, obtaining their colour from the Islamic-style Tunisian flag. An all-white fin displays the company's ingenious 'TA' logo with a gap in the letter 'A' formed by a small white leaping Gazelle. Black 'Tunis Air' titles give precedence to the English version on the starboard side, and Arabic on the port.

Airbus Industrie A300B4 TS-IMA. (Norbert Heck)

TURK HAVA YOLLARI - THY

THY had been operating under the name of Devlet Hava Yollari for over twenty years when in February 1956 the airline became a private corporation. Today, scheduled passenger and cargo services link Turkey with major cities throughout Europe and in Africa and the Middle East, and domestic flights connect seventeen Turkish cities.

Nine Boeing 727-200s and nine McDonnell Douglas DC-9-30s form the nucleus of the THY fleet with two McDonnell Douglas DC-10-10s used for long haul and high density services, supplemented by seven Airbus Industrie A310s. Domestic flights use two Fokker Fellowships and three DHC-7s, with the two Boeing 707-321Cs employed solely for pure freight services.

The current THY livery is composed of the red and white national colours, in a stylish pinstripe form. Five narrow red lines form the cheatline, separating the white upper fuselage from the grey undersides, and terminate in a distinctive black anti-dazzle panel at the nose. A band of six broad stripes covers most of the tail fin interrupted only by a white disk displaying the traditional THY bird logo. An unusually long title arrangement takes-up most of the upper fuselage with the black letters reading 'Turk Hava Yollari - Turkish Airlines THY' followed by the national flag; the Turkish version appearing before the English on both sides. It was speculated that a new livery would be introduced with the first A310s in mid-1985, but they were eventually delivered in the same traditional colourscheme.

Airbus Industrie A310 TC - JCL at Zurich (Antonio Branca)

TYROLEAN AIRWAYS

Based at Innsbruck in Western Austria, Tyrolean was known as Aircraft Innsbruck from its formation in 1958 until 1979 when the present title was adopted. Scheduled passenger services link Innsbruck with Vienna, Salzburg and Graz in Austria and reach Zurich (Switzerland) and Frankfurt (West Germany). Inclusive tours, ad-hoc charters, ambulance flights and air-taxi services are also operated.

The fleet consists of three Canadian-built STOL transports, two 50-seat DHC-7s and a new 36-seat DHC-8.

When, in mid-1985, Tyrolean decided to update its image, the company was already using a livery widely regarded as one of the most attractive in Europe. The new identity retained the red, orange and yellow colouring, although their shades had been altered slightly, making the red and orange darker and the yellow brighter. An all-white fuselage now displays the triple cheatlines in diagonal form on the rear fuselage, tail and engines with titles still in black on the tail and forward lower fuselage. As with other 'diagonal' liveries, the registration appears within the cheatline sloping accordingly.

De Havilland Canada DHC-8 OE-HLR (Adolfo Tagliabue)

UNITED AIRLINES

United is the largest airline in the western world and offers a vast network of scheduled domestic passenger services to all major cities in the United States. International services are also flown to points in Canada, Bahamas, Mexico, Japan and Hong Kong as well as worldwide charters.

The present fleet numbers some 350 jet airliners comprising Boeing 727s, 737s, 747s and 767s and McDonnell Douglas DC-8s, MD-82s and DC-10s.

Patriotic red and blue colouring is used for the large 'U' tail motif and for the main cheatlines, brightened by a third line in orange. The 'U' logo is repeated after the black 'United' fuselage lettering. Most aircraft in the fleet sport a white upper and lower fuselage finish although some have a natural metal lower half.

Boeing 767-222 N608UA at Chicago (Ron Kluk)

UNITED PARCELS SERVICE - UPS

UPS is one of several major airlines offering coast-to-coast overnight small parcels services within the United States, with its main hub located at Louisville, Kentucky. All flights are operated on behalf of UPS by other carriers under contract, including Orion Air, Evergreen International, Interstate and SAT-Air.

Aircraft operated for UPS presently include twenty-seven Boeing 727s, six Boeing 747s, fourteen McDonnell Douglas DC-8s (-73CFs and -61CFs) and eleven turboprop Swearingen Expediters.

Unique amonst major airlines in using chocolate brown as a predominant colour, the UPS livery comprises a conventional broad windowline which ultimately covers the whole tail-fin. The company logo, a shield displaying 'UPS' lettering beneath a 'wrapped parcel' appears on the tail in gold outline, and bold brown 'United Parcel Service' lettering is carried on the forward upper fuselage.

Boeing 747-123F/SCD N672UP at Ontario. (Mickey Bednar)

UNION DE TRANSPORTS AERIENS - UTA

UTA was formed on October 1st 1963 through the amalgamation of UAT and TAI. Today the company is a major French airline offering passenger and freight services connecting France with Africa, the Far East, Australasia and the United States, as well as operating local services in the South Pacific area.

The current all wide-body UTA fleet consists of six McDonnell Douglas DC-10s and five Boeing 747s, two of which are pure freighters, and one is a -300 series stretched upper deck.

UTA was one of the first airlines to adopt the modern white overall fuselage colouring, which in this case features passenger doors highlighted in bright green. The whole fin and rearmost part of the fuselage is in dark blue, with the small white 'UTA' logo appearing inconspicuously at the top of the tail. Vast fuselage titles in dark blue are so large that they are often readable from the ground on overflying aircraft. Pure freight aircraft have an all-white fuselage without green highlights, but wear additional blue cargo titles.

Boeing 747-3B3 F-GDUA.

VARIG

Varig's history can be traced back over fifty years to its formation in May 1927 to operate a single Dornier WAL flying boat over the domestic Porto Alegre-Rio Grande route, succeeding the earlier Kondor Syndikat. Within thirty-five years the company had expanded to such a degree that it was in a position to take-over the REAL consortium making it the largest airline in South America, a position it still holds. The present scheduled route system includes both passenger and freight services throughout the region and to Europe, South Africa, the Far East, Central America and the United States.

Twelve McDonnell Douglas DC-10-30s and three Boeing 747-200s, soon to be joined by two 747-300s, are used on long-haul routes, with Boeing 707s, 727s and 737s and Airbus Industrie A300s flown regionally; twelve Lockheed Electra turboprops are still employed on domestic and short-haul sectors.

The predominant dark blue is obtained from the national flag and colours the broad cheatline, which curves round under the aircraft's chin and also features a 'seam' effect created by white pinstripes at windowlevel. The famous compass logo is displayed on the fin above black 'Varig' titles, but on the fuselage the company name is repeated in blue alongside the Brazilian flag and 'Brasil' lettering in black. The livery is slightly adapted to fit the shapes of other aircraft in the fleet with the only notable variation being the application of the 'flying figurehead' logo above the cheatline on the 747s but within it on all other types. Underside colours vary with those of the 747s and most DC-10s in natural metal, the A300s in grey and some DC-10s in a more attractive white.

Boeing 747-2L5B PP-VNB at Frankfurt. (Richard Vandervord)

VIRGIN ATLANTIC

Virgin Atlantic was formed in June 1984 by Richard Branson, chairman of the Virgin Group, to offer low-fare scheduled passenger services between London Gatwick and New York-Newark. A feeder service was later added, using initially a leased BIA British Aerospace One-eleven, later replaced by a British Air Ferries Viscount, to connect Maastricht in Holland with the London end of the transatlantic service

The Virgin Atlantic Boeing 747, which is the only aircraft to ever carry the full company livery, wears a scheme which although it is clean and fresh, at first glance does not appear particularly unusual. A simple orange 'straight-through' windowline extends below the similarly-coloured 'Virgin' signature near the cockpit windows, and repeated in white on the all-orange fin, but also on the tail appears a comical 'after-thought' which in some detail portrays one of the painters almost falling off his platform, complete with tea-mug and portable radio and splashing paint from his falling tin down the rear part of the fuselage.

Boeing 747-287B G-VIRG at London-Heathrow Airport. (Chris Green)

VIASA

In January 1961, the Venezuelan Government rationalised the country's air services by forming VIASA to take over the international routes of Avensa and LAV, although Avensa retained a 25% stake in the new company. Scheduled passenger and freight operations commenced in April of that year and now reach across the Atlantic to major cities in Europe, as well as numerous points in the USA, Central America, South America and the Caribbean.

Six McDonnell Douglas DC-10-30s are flown on long-haul and high-density routes, supplemented by regional McDonnell Douglas DC-8-63s, MD-82s and a DC-9-33.

The very latest Viasa livery includes two minor alterations to the traditional image that has been displayed by the company for some years. The new blue cheatline follows modern trends and now appears below the windows allowing for an extended white cabin roof to effectively brighten the scheme, and the somewhat disjointed 'seven stars' are now ommitted from behind the cockpit windows allowing the orange 'Viasa' logo to move forward into a more prominent position. Blue 'Venezuela' lettering is displayed over the wings, another forward move, but the characteristic orange fin remains unchanged, with its white 'Viasa' logo and Venezuelan flag near the top of the rudder.

McDonnell Douglas DC-10 YV-137C at Orly in May 1985. (Luc Bereni)

WARDAIR

Wardair takes its name from its original founder, Maxwell W. Ward, who started the airline in 1952 to take over the operations of the Polaris Charter Company, which he had also formed, some six years earlier. Initial charter services used a de Havilland Canada Otter and were mostly flown within the Arctic regions of Canada, but in 1962 Wardair entered the lucrative trans-Atlantic charter market. The company now flies passenger charters worldwide but mainly to Europe, the United States and the Caribbean.

The modest wide-bodied fleet consists of four Boeing 747s (two series -100s and two series -200s) and three McDonnell Douglas DC-10-30s.

Large 'Wardair' titling in dark blue dominates the forward upper fuselage, immediately behind which, commences the red upper cheatline, gradually widening as it proceeds along the fuselage and sweeping up onto the tail where it is interrupted to accommodate similarly-styled 'Wardair Canada' lettering. Note that the tail lettering is carried on the centre engine of the DC-10 and consequently comparatively lower on the fin than the 747. The white upper fuselage and natural metal undersides are separated by a narrow blue below-window stripe which extends along the entire fuselage length, parallel to the upper red line but maintaining its width.

Boeing 747-1D1 C-FDJC at Newcastle. (Glenn Auld)

WORLDWAYS CANADA

Worldways has expanded considerably over the ten years since its formation in 1974 as a domestic Canadian charter airline operating a single piston-engined Douglas DC-4. Today, all-jet passenger and freight charter services are offered on both a domestic and international basis, particularly to Europe.

Four McDonnell Douglas DC-8-63s were acquired from CP Air in March 1983 and are now used exclusively, replacing the earlier Boeing 707s.

The new DC-8s are painted in an identical livery to that of their 707 predecessors with a narrow double cheatline in two values of blue extending from the nose to a point at the rear where it sweeps up almost vertically just 'clipping' the lower leading edge of the fin. An intricate light blue-outlined globe is displayed on the all-white tail combining with a dark blue superimposed 'W' initial to form the company's motif and large 'Worldways' titling in the same dark blue is displayed on the forward upper fuselage succeeded by secondary, much smaller, 'Canada' lettering.

McDonnell Douglas DC-8-63 C-FCPQ. (J.F. Blatherwick)

XP EXPRESS PARCELS SYSTEMS

XP Express was formed in January 1982 to offer a small parcels services between Maastricht (Holland) and Luton (England) initially using a leased Piper Aztec. The company's Maastricht operations base is now linked with several European points including Basle, Milan, Luton, Rotterdam, Amsterdam, Hamburg and Copenhagen.

Fleet mainstay is in the shape of six Piper Navajo Chieftains although a Britten-Norman Trislander, Cessna 414A and flagship Fokker Friendship are also operated.

Dynamically-styled, the XP Express colourscheme employs a pure white fuselage 'setting-off' the twin diagonal bands in bold shades of yellow and green which embrace the rear-fuselage section and most of the tail fin. All lettering is in black from the bold 'stencilled' 'XP' logo to the 'Express Parcel Systems' subtitles, individual aircraft name and registration. Note the black nose radome and anti-dazzle panel.

Fokker Friendship PH-FKT. (Richard Vandervord)

YEMANIA - YEMEN AIRWAYS

The national airline of the Yeman Arab Republic was formed in 1954 and was known as Yemen Airlines until September 1972. Initial operations were undertaken using Douglas DC-3s to connect several domestic points and also to fly international services across the Red Sea to Djibouti. Today the company provides scheduled passenger services linking the capital Sana'a with destinations in Europe, the Middle East, Africa and Asia as well as linking major domestic communities.

Two modern airliner types have been chosen for long-range and domestic services respectively, the Boeing 727 and De Havilland Canada DHC-7.

An extremely smart scheme employs twin broad cheatlines in complimentary shades of bright red and royal blue to disect the fresh all-white fuselage finish. The tail fin displays a curious company motif which comprises a stylised wing section with three trailing streaks passing behind an Islamic red crescent. Titling is in dark blue and reads 'Yemenia Yemen Airways' followed by its Arabic equivalent with the English lettering given precedence on both sides.

Boeing 727-2N8 4W-ACH at Paris. (Christian Laugier)

ZAS AIRLINES OF EGYPT

ZAS Airlines of Egypt was formed in June 1982 as a venture into the airline business by the Zakarni Group, a major Egyptian import-export organisation. Worldwide freight charters are currently offered in addition to a scheduled London-Cairo connection, although the company has also been granted authority to offer passenger charters and helicopter operations to support the Egyptian oil industry.

The present fleet consists of four pure-freight Boeing 707s which were originally delivered to BOAC and Air France in the late sixties/early seventies.

The white fuselage colouring projects a clean modern image over which run dual cheatlines in medium and royal blue. A bold blue 'Z' initial dominates the white fin, emphasised by shadowing in the lighter colour, and appears above deep blue 'Zakarni' lettering in Arabic on both sides. A winged 'ZAS' motif in red is located on the upper fuselage above the wing-root and is flanked by blue 'Airline of Egypt' subtitles in Arabic and English, mirrored on the opposite side so that the English translation always appears at the front of the aircraft.

Boeing 707-328C SU-DAA. (J.V.D. Heijden)

INDEX